I0420215

UNDER ORION

HUNTING STORIES

From Appalachia to Africa

Richard Mann

FOR BAT

May he continue to live the hunter's life under the stars of Orion.

Under Orion, Hunting Stories, From Appalachia To Africa, Copyright ©
2015 by Ramworks INC. All rights reserved, including the right to
reproduce this book or portions thereof, in any form or by any means,
electronic or mechanical, including photocopying, recording, or by
any information storage and retrieval system, without permission
in writing from the publisher. All inquiries should be addressed to:

Ramworks INC.
Shadowland Publishing
3702 Rocky Branch Road
Princeton, West Virginia 24740

Mann, Richard

First Edition

ISBN (13): 978-1517463045
ISBN (10): 1517463041

ACKNOWLEDGEMENTS

This book could not have been possible without the many hunting companions I've had through the years. If you've shared a campfire with me, you have contributed to this book. There are simply too many names to list.

However, I cannot allow you to read any further without acknowledging the three most important influences in a life that has made this book possible.

My parents were constant supporters of my addiction to the outdoors and firearms. Beyond that, when I resigned my position as a Railroad Detective, they continued to lend encouragement. Even though they were sure I'd stepped on a banana peel.

My grandfather was my hillbilly educator. He never made it past third grade but became a successful businessman and was even a member of the Board of Education in his later years. He died when I was 14 but was with me through the very formative years that have made me what I am and always will be.

I am a hillbilly through and through. I'm proud of it and I'm proud of those who contributed to my mountain ways. These stories are as much a reflection of those who shaped me as they are of the enjoyment and education I've experienced outside.

At first, with them by my side and later on, with them watching over me from some rugged mountian top far, far away.

CONTENTS

Prologue - Under Orion

Just a child, lost in the adventure and captivated by the vastness of a darkened forest, I became a hunter. Maybe, because of the respect I had for him or because he was my friend, it was mostly Grandpa who lit the pilot light for the fire that now burns in my hunter's heart. He had "Old Buck," a mixed-breed hound that was my friend. In truth I was less than a child and the first excursions predate my memory but it was chasing coonhounds under the stars where I became.

The question of the hunter is often debated. Is a hunter a manifestation of environment or simply a genetic guarantee like baldness and beauty? In truth it is a needless debate. The constellation Orion, positioned on the celestial equator, looks over us all from the peaks of Montana to the green hills of Africa. Orion is visible in both the northern and southern hemispheres, from every inhabited place on Earth and his mystical legend goes back to the Second Millennium. The first humans hunted under his watch and for centuries since, hunting has insured our existence.

Hunting is an instinctive human activity. In truth we all hunt. Humans are hunters and gatherers. My wife braves the grocery store scrum for fruit, vegetables, and meat while I slip my way to the field, then trudge home in the darkness under Orion's gaze. Hunting is in us all. A genetic code trapped in the helix spiral of DNA embedded so deep neither time nor technology can separate it from our bits and pieces. It is the link to the survival of the human species and the means to insure one of our basic needs: nourishment.

I found Orion very young, long before formal education learned me on celestial science. Orion and his hunting dog, Sirius, are the masters of the winter skies. As a young coon hunter they not only kept me company on many a dark night but also showed me the way home. From late fall, when the bucks antlers are ivory white and hard, until early spring when the wild turkey's gobble cracks the foggy dawn, Orion rises in the night to celebrate with the hunter his take.

Those darkened quests with Grandpa, parents, family, and friends were where Orion cast his spell on me. Now, mostly, it's the whitetail buck that I seek. For his flesh will nourish my family, his hide will make my coat, and his antlers will decorate my wall just as Orion decorates the skies of the season of pursuit. As Orion climbs from the horizon and as blackness engulfs my walk home from the timber, I think of the nature I have experienced and the other hunters I have shared the field with.

To quote the Star Splitter by Robert Frost:

"You know Orion always comes up sideways.
Throwing his leg over our fence of mountains,
And rising on his hands, he looks in on me…"

Legend has it that Orion boasted of skill so great he could kill all the animals of earth. Those boasts were likely the seed of our familiar "hunter's yarn" which is shared around countless campfires and is only loosely based on the truth. It's how a six point becomes a ten point and a 75-yard shot becomes 200.

It was Gaea, the Greek Mythology Goddess of Earth, who would be the end of Orion. Fearing that one day he might carry out his boasts, Gaea sent a giant scorpion to sting Orion. And therein lies the true lesson of conservation that Orion teaches us. Take only what you need and boast only in jest at the edge of the campfire, for it is excessiveness in either tale or take that is the enemy of the hunter.

The scorpion stung Orion on his heel where the mighty star Rigel, the seventh brightest star in the sky is located, and the great hunter died. Both Orion and the scorpion were given honored, but opposite, places in the heavens where they would never meet again. As Orion slips behind one horizon, the scorpion rises on the other.

Yes, hunting is in us all. The true question is when or if it will come out and in what manner it will manifest itself. Will you pursue the mallard or the moose, the turkey or the elk, or the whitetail deer? Some seem drawn to the timber from birth while it takes others half a lifetime to find it. My wife did not start hunting until she was in her mid 40s. The seed is there, waiting for the proper water to help it grow.

Some will argue hunting is a thing of the past, that humans no longer need to engage in blood sport for survival. These poor souls are lost in the fog and cannot see the stars for the clouds. For while we for sure hunt because it is fun, there is something else that drives us to rise in the darkness, suffer the bone chilling cold, and spend our vacations somewhere other than Disneyland. Humans are social creatures and pack animals. Humans are hunters. Hunting is not a tradition some try to hold on to in the face of technology and sophistication, it is a natural activity for our species.

As you struggle to drag your buck back to camp in the gloom of evening, look to the heavens. Find the belt of the hunter. Find his raised bow and understand he is hunting; the bear, the bull and all the other starry animals. Thank him for unlocking your genetic code and letting the hunter in you escape. Let him know you understand the lesson and whether for sport or food, no more than is necessary is what you will take. For while you sit by the campfire warming your body and the venison you found, you will be where all hunters should forever be - under Orion.

What do you hunt, Orion,

This starry night?

The ram, the bull and the Lion,

And the great Bear, says Orion,

With my starry quiver and beautiful belt

I am trying to find a good thick pelt

To warm my shoulders tonight,

To warm my shoulders tonight.

Author Unknown

1 - A GOOD START

He came as the fog begin to lift. Just as silent and with the same stealth; materializing like a vampire from an old black and white picture show. Feet silent on the forest floor, he paused for a moment just shy of the water's edge and then crossed the small stream. He stopped at the base of an old weathered, hollowed out oak and surveyed his surroundings like a shoplifter preparing to make the grab. He was old and wise but had no idea I was there. Comfortable he had not betrayed the location of his den, the old bore coon eased up the tree and into its hollow sanctuary.

Like his disappearance was the Sun's cue, it peaked over the crest of the ridge. It was deer time.

As I set there, perched above the ground and anchored to the side of a tall white pine. My mind drifted back to my beginnings as a hunter. Both of my parents were avid raccoon hunters. They enjoyed the cool fall nights, the music of the hounds, and each other's companionship. In the fall, three months before I was born, I was coon hunting. An old wife's tale postulates that to insure a bitch hound's hunting instinct is passed on to her pups they must be marked. You "mark" pups by putting a coon out to their mother while she still carries them. So, "marked" I must be.

My first hunting experience was chasing Dad, running ahead of Mom, following behind our hounds. This was a long time long ago when you couldn't find good hunting clothes or boots for a five-year-old boy. Our coon hunts were a family affair. Aunts, uncles, cousins, and grandparents all participated and when the old folks were not laughing or cussing the hounds, us kids were their amusement.

Soon, Mom introduced me to bushytails with a .22. Then, Dad showed me how much more effective a shotgun could be on rowdy tree rats. A whitetail doe was my first big game trophy; found, shot, and dressed without adult supervision. I vividly remember the look on my father's face when I walked into camp smiling, with hands still bloody and trembling. My folks nor anyone else I knew back then bowhunted. But to a young impressionable boy, Robin Hood and the Green Arrow fueled a pilot light that has burned to this day. Just as they did with all my other interests, Mom and Dad lent vital support and encouragement. All this before I ever kissed a girl.

Now, 25 years later, I often find myself back in those same woods, hunting in places where nighttime and other adolescent hunting adventures from long ago occurred. It may be a particular hollow or ridge, or maybe a creek crossing or a big rock. But, littered throughout the woods around our hunting camp are memories from my early outdoor education. It is a treasure to sit on stand at a place where something special once happened. Places where you learned things. Things about the wild. And, just as importantly, things about yourself and other people.

Drunken with memories I almost let him get too close. His approach, like the raccoon's, was silent. As I fought to return to the world of right now, my heart rate quickened when I realized the company I now had under me. At 15 feet he stopped, chest behind a tree. I could hear him breathe and see the steam of his breath curl up around his magnificent antlers. Bow in hand, I eased to my feet. One step and he would clear the tree, expose his engine room, and open a path for my cedar shaft.

My bow hand was shaking in a completely different rhythm from the rest of my body. With my breathing shallow and fast I wondered what the buck would hear first: my feeble attempts to feed my oxygen starved lungs or my heart trying to supply my muscles with the oxygen I could not gasp. I'll never know if it was the roar of my body trying to cope with the adrenalin rush or my putrid human odor. The buck realized things were not as they should be. Spinning around, he bounded out to 20 yards.

He turned broadside with his head erect and ears forward; standing as arrogant as a king and looking right at me as if to say, "You are an intruder, you do not belong!"

My training had paid off. My childhood of adventure and excitement was actually a free education of things that are wild. Like a momma wolf teaches her pups to hunt, I had been trained as a predator. Trained to know where to look for sign and how to read it once it's found. To learn my prey, to be where they are going before they get there, and encroach into their space before they realize I don't belong.

My bow was up and my finger touched the corner of my mouth. Hesitating for an instant, as always just before release, a thought flashed before the arrow left on its way. I had definitely been given a good start.

2 - BAT's DEER

Bat went on his first deer hunt when he was four years old. It wasn't a deer hunt most hunters would brag about or even admit they went on. We rode the four-wheeler about a half-mile from camp, parked in a little hollow, and walked up on a ridge. The ground was partially covered with that wet slushy snow kids like to play in and that's what Bat did; leaving foot prints and kicking the slush.

We sat together under a big white oak at the edge of a grown up field. Bat scanned the timber with the binoculars and intermittently blew a grunt call. He wasn't still or quite and I would have been just as surprised to see Bigfoot as a deer.

In about ten minutes Bat asked, "Can we go somewhere else?"

"Sure." I said. "Where you wanna go?"

"Can we go up there?" Bat asked, pointing at a dilapidated rail fence about 30 yards up the ridge. "I bet we'll see a deer up there."

We moved up the hill, hunkered in amongst the old split rails like spies. Bat continued his grunting and scanning with the binoculars. It wasn't long before he wanted to move again so we got back on the ATV and repeated similar set-ups for the next hour or so. We never saw a deer but Bat bragged about his hunt to his Grandpa when we got back to camp, telling the tale just like the adult hunters when they trudged in after a full day in the woods.

The following week my friend Charlie Sisk came up from Texas to hunt with me and I was telling him how I needed a rifle sized for a young boy. Charlie was looking at a shelf of ammunition behind the counter in an old grocery store when he saw a box of .25-35 ammo. That's when the idea hit him that a lightweight rifle chambered for that cartridge would be just about right for boy. About six months later Charlie sent Bat a downsized Remington model 788 in .25-35.

Bat didn't have the arm strength to shoot the rifle off-hand but from the bench he had no trouble keeping his shots inside a circle the size of a snuff can at 50 yards. He was excited about the upcoming deer season and exuded an Alvin York confidence is his ability to shoot.

Opening morning was bitter cold. We only had a couple days to hunt and even though the mercury hung around the zero mark, Bat managed to sit, tucked in between my legs, during several outings. The binoculars had lost some of their fascination but the grunt call kept him entertained. The cold crept in and we had to move regularly to keep warm. Our few days soon passed and so did another year without Bat seeing a deer.

That summer we timbered some of our hunting property to create better habitat. We also placed a few ladder stands. Bat became involved in the process, picking out the one he wanted to hunt from. I figured this would be helpful because the tree house atmosphere would lend some intrigue to the hunt and the safety rail would provide a good rest for the rifle.

When I woke Bat well before daylight on opening day I expected it would be a chore to roust him. He crawled right out, got into his hunting clothes and hurried down stairs where his Pa had breakfast waiting.

"You going deer hunting?" his Pa asked.

"I'm gonna shoot a buck." Bat replied in a matter of fact manner and we started out the trail. I had the rifle and Bat had the flashlight. At age six a kid will find more fascination in a flashlight than a gun. The stand Bat had picked was only about a quarter mile from camp and we were situated well before daylight; the back porch light on the cabin just visible through the trees. Bat was prepared; he brought his Nintendo GameBoy along and played with it - with the sound muted - until color began to find the forest.

Bat was attentive for about an hour and then as some of his adrenalin subsided he began to feel the chill of the morning air. He leaned against me and shut his eyes. That's when I saw the buck. It stepped out along the far edge of the clear cut and was picking at fallen acorns along the perimeter. I whispered to Bat just like they do on those TV hunting shows and he got behind his rifle. He was sitting on my knee and I could feel the excitement coursing through his body.

"Can I shoot?" He whispered.

"Wait. That's a long ways. He'll feed down into this little draw and come up right beside us." It was about 100 yards and though I had confidence in Bat's shooting, he'd never tried to shoot when he was this excited. And, I didn't want to stack the deck against him for his first real opportunity.

The buck did just as I suspected. Bat began to relax and scolded me for not letting him shoot. "I had the X right on his shoulder Dad. Why didn't you let me shoot?" His frustration was apparent.

"He'll come out right there. Just be patient." I hoped I was right.
About ten minutes later I saw the buck picking his way out of the draw just as I expected. I pointed him out to Bat and got his rifle orientated in the right direction. It had been our plan to let Bat rest the rifle over a glove, across the safety rail. In our excitement that was forgotten and now he was lined up on the buck with the rifle resting on my forearm. The range was about sixty yards and both of us were shaking.

"When he stops shoot him right in the shoulder." I whispered. Bat said nothing.

The buck stopped, raised his head and looked our way. I'm guessing he heard both of our hearts pounding. "Shoot." I whispered, desperately trying to keep my shakes and the excitement in my voice from interfering with Bat's aim.

I watched the buck and I watched the end of the rifle barrel gyrating around like a whip antenna on a state trooper's car. I could feel Bat adjusting his body against mine as he tried to line up the sights. Finally, Bat pulled the trigger and before it even registered with me that the buck had been hit, Bat yelled, "I got him!" Sure enough, the buck lunged forward, stumbled, and piled up in a blow down.

The elation was tremendous and I immediately had to shift my focus from the hunt to keep Bat and I from falling out of the ladder stand as we celebrated. I wanted to scream out; Bat did. We climbed down and went to the deer. There was a humble though slightly smug smile on Bat's face as he looked at the buck.

"We're going to eat him, right?" Bat asked.

"Oh yeah, we'll eat him." I replied as I patted him on the back. "Go back to camp and get your Pa. Tell him to bring the Gator to haul your deer back." No sooner than the words left my mouth Bat was gone in a flat out run toward camp.

Hunter's like telling their stories. It's not so much bragging as it is the sharing of an interaction with nature. It's that interaction that creates the stir inside the hunter, which is a sensation we are compelled to seek out and share.

Bat told his to story to his Granny and Pa in the same camp where I had told my stories to them and my grandparents. Every hunter makes each story their own and Bat was no different. After he recounted the events as they happened he added a bit at the end:

"It was sixty yards through the heart Pa. But I don't know why Dad wouldn't let me shoot when we first saw the buck. I could have hit him easy."

Kids!

3 - THE BOBCAT BLUES

I'm not a very good storyteller. I think this is mostly because I have such an affinity for the truth and often the truth does not make that good of a story. This lack of ability or maybe desire to embellish may come from 13 years of writing police incident reports where, "Just the facts ma'am." was expected. The old cliché goes, truth can be stranger than fiction and in this case it is. I couldn't have made this up if I tried.

Our tale starts in South Texas near Pearsall. This was supposed to be one of those fancy media hunts where the sponsors arrange first rate accommodations in an area saturated with critters and provide fine shooting firearms with plenty of ammunition. Well, two out of four is what we got. Remington supplied several nice rifles and lots of ammo. As for our accommodations, we were housed in an old farmhouse with paint peeling off the walls and flea infested furniture.

We were hunting feral hogs, coyotes, and bobcats. After four days of hard hunting by six of us, our take amounted to two bobcats, two coyotes, and three hogs. The hogs had been hunted so hard the only reliable way to see one was with a spotlight. As for the coyotes, well, I found two tracks in four days. One I'll admit was moderately fresh. The others were so old I think they were fossilized relics.

But this story is not about how fly by night outfitters can take advantage of companies looking to gain some press on their products. Still, if I may, let me interject something. If you arrive at the lodge and find no "grab and grin" photos on the wall, that's a clue. If the shooting range amounts to two, 50-pound bags of corn, thrown over a folding card table, that's another clue. If after two days of hard hunting and seeing no coyotes your outfitter begins to spout stories of all the coyotes he saw on the ride out to pick you up, that's another clue. And finally, if the only critter sign you see amounts to petrified poop and crusty old tracks, you do not need anymore clues.

If you have come to the conclusion that I considered the outfitter and the country we were hunting to be dreadful, then you reached the same conclusion all those in attendance had come to. The hunt could have been described as a "goat roping" or maybe, just simply, a disaster. Except for one thing: the bob cat.

Few will argue that Bill Bynum was one of the foremost experts on predator hunting and calling in the world. I had wanted to hunt with Bill for a long time and was glad he was present at this fiasco. The evening of the first day Bill said, "Boy, grab your gear. We're going to go kill a bob cat."

The outfitter drove us about a mile from the house and dropped us off along a brushy creek. As the guide, no let me re-phrase that, as the man piloting the truck disappeared, Bill whispered to sit down and be still. He lit up a cigarette and keenly watched the wind carry the smoke away as he pried into the thick brush with his eyes that had been trained in the Tennessee backwoods.

"We're gonna go right down next to the creek and set up. Be ready, don't move a muscle. Them cats spook if you blink." Bill whispered as he crushed out his cigarette and placed the butt in his pocket. I followed along behind him down the trail and he motioned for me to set up at the base of a crooked oak, indicating the direction I should watch. Bill arranged himself behind me, facing opposite, and we both became one with the woods.

As I became immersed in my surroundings, wondering how many skeeters it would take to drain enough blood from me to cause unconsciousness, Bill let out a squall on his predator call and a chill shot down my spine and ended up in my feet. This casued me to jerk like 10,000 volt's had just been pushed through me. Bill cast an evil eye my direction.

Ten seconds later I looked up and this bobcat was charging me. It stopped just across the path at about 20 feet with its eyes boring into my soul. I knew a slow deliberate movement of the rifle would be fraught with disaster so with all the dexterity and speed I could muster, I swung the rifle on the cat and when the reticle covered fur. I pulled the trigger. Bill had not seen the cat and the roar of the .221 Fireball lifted not just his feet, but his ass, off the ground.

"What was it?" Bill shouted.

"Bob cat!" I screamed in a whisper.

"Did you get him?" Bill asked as gravity finally pulled his body back to earth.

"Yep. But the hit may not be good. He didn't give me much time."

We ambled on over to the spot where the cat had been when I fired and found blood and hair. "He won't go far. Let's give him a minute and think this out." Bill said as he pulled a cigarette from his pocket. Bill's first step in sorting anything out, be it trailing up a wounded bobcat or preparing for a tax audit, is to smoke a cigarette.

Two cigarettes later we took up the blood trail and in 30 yards we reached the steep bank of the creek where the blood stopped. The bank was about 20 feet above water and there was a deep under-cut on our side. Bill, being the cat killing expert he is, surmised the wounded feline was hiding underneath the under-cut waiting in ambush. Just as I was beginning to get the picture that I was going to have to be the one to go over the bank first, Bill said, "There's your cat."

Bill was pointing up into a huge, slanted oak tree that hung out over the creek. And there, on a limb, staring at us belligerently, was my bobcat.

"I believe he is hurt bad." Bill said pulling another cigarette from the chest pocket of his camo shirt. And I knew, then and there, he was preparing to calculate our next move. "If you shoot him this close you'll ruin your pelt. I bet if we just wait a bit he'll die there on that limb and you can crawl right up there and get him." Three cigarettes later that cat was still there, opening his eyes every so often to give us that malicious glare.

"I've had enough of this shit!" Bill blurted as he picked up a stick and hurled it at the cat. He missed but the cat fell out of the tree and into the rushing water. "He'll drown now." At first I thought Bill was right but the old cat just kept flopping and squalling as he tried to make it to the bank on the other side. Finally he did. I watched through my riflescope as the cat lay completely motionless with his head resting on the bank. That's when Bill had what I am sure he would consider, a good idea at the time.

"Get a good stick, sneak around to the other side of the creek, and go get your cat. I'm sure he is dead. He ain't moving. But take a stick just in case. I'll stay here and watch him with the rifle." Bill grinned, found him a stump and planted his lanky frame, indicating the topic was closed for discussion.

As luck would have it, the only stick I could find with enough rigidity to even swat a fly was about four feet long and five inches in diameter. We're talking a log or at least firewood here. I wasn't too concerned though, it would take me about 20 minutes to navigate to the other creek bank and by then I doubted I would need a stick at all.

When I reached the other side Bill yelled that the cat had not moved and he felt certain he was dead. I started the decent down the steep muddy bank and on my second step, slipped. When I came to a stop my feet were at the bob cat's face which was no longer resting on the bank waiting for rigor mortise to set in.

"YeeeeOwwww!." Squalled the bob cat. "YeeeeOwwww!" I echoed repeatedly as I began to frail the creek bank, water, and my entire surroundings with a wooden club that looked like some weapon from the dark ages. Finally, I connected and the melee stopped.

I was wet and winded when Bill shouted more advice across the creek. I thought Bill had said to hold him under water with the stick but I wasn't sure. Mostly because Bill had been overcome with a fit of laughter that had consumed his entire body. This of course explains why he was flopping around on the other creek bank like a possessed, camouflaged clown. Had it been necessary for him to shoot in amongst us to save me from a serious mauling, he would have been incapable.

I pushed the cat under the water until no more bubbles reached the surface. I timed it, waiting three minutes. Bill, now somewhat recovered from his diabolical laughing fit, said, "You got him now boy! Get him out of the water and let's go get another one." I started to reach down and pick up the cat when something in the back of my mind said. "Self, this is not a good idea. Make sure the cat is dead before you pick it up." So, I leaned over and flipped the bobcat on his sopping wet ear with my finger.

"YeeeOwww!" said the cat.

The expletives that began to roll from my mouth would have embarrassed me even in a roadhouse, but they were drowned out by Bill's second uncontrollable episode of laughter. The bank was too steep to run up, my stick was floating down the creek, and I was weaponless. So, with no alternative, I grabbed the cat in a death grip around the neck with both hands and shoved him deep into the mud under the water. I stood there, knee deep in the creek, choking a bobcat while my hunting partner wiped crocodile tears of laughter as he continually repeated, "Let him go, I'm sure he's dead now!"

Ten minutes later I climbed out of the creek with my bobcat. This was my first "called-up cat" and I decided if they were all like this, as far as I was concerned this one would be my last. And that's the truth!

4 - THE FENCE

The kudu has been described as the grey ghost of Africa. The long spiraling horns and the elusiveness of this antelope has made it one of the most sought after big game trophies in the world. I was on my fifth African safari before I ever looked through a riflescope at a kudu bull. When I did, I had seven to choose from. But, there was a problem.

Some say fences have no place in hunting and look down upon others who hunt behind them, arguing it's not a fair chase endeavor. As a firearms and hunting journalist I have an obligation to experience all forms of hunting. I've hunted behind high fences in South Africa that encircled more than 25,000 acres and I've hunted behind zoo-like fenced compounds in the United States not much larger than a feedlot. I prefer pursuits not confined by fences, but that's not always possible.

It was the last day of a seven-day hunt and I was with Geoffrey Wayland of Fort Richmond Safaris. The Wayland property encompasses about 60,000 acres. Half is behind an eight-foot high fence and is reserved for hunting. The other half is behind a three-foot fence and is a working sheep and cattle farm.

Just south of Fort Richmond is the Orange River and kudu bulls were moving up from this river - in and around the Wayland's property -

looking for love and affection. The rut was wide open and Geoffrey and I were spending the evening looking for a bull, who was looking for a one night stand.

We were working along a low ridge, periodically stopping and glassing the draws and flatlands when Geoffrey's lead tracker, Steven, informed us he'd located a group of kudu on a hill to our west. We worked in under a large acacia tree to have a look, and there they were. About six hundred yards across open grassland we could see numerous kudu courting on the hillside. We counted nine cows and seven bulls; two of the bulls were dandies. I asked Geoffrey if he had a plan.

"Not really." Geoffrey paused. "Those kudu are on my neighbor's farm. You see that cattle fence running up the valley? They'll have to jump that before we can take one."

"You're kidding?" I mumbled. "You mean in South Africa, the land of high fence concessions, a three foot cattle fence is standing between me and a free range kudu?" Geoffrey smiled so I looked at Steven for some glimmer of hope. Steven smiled too and said, "They will jump."

"Before dark? I asked.

He nodded and said, "Yes." with what appeared to be the same confidence he had in the setting sun. One word when I needed a paragraph of encouragement.

We began our move to the base of the hill. We ran through an open area and nearing the flatland we came upon a dry creek bed. I went first, low crawling through thorns. Geoffrey slipped up behind me and Steven brought up the rear. We had remained undetected and assumed a prone position. It was about two and a half hours until dark and the kudu bulls were pushing the cows downhill and into the bottom. But, they were moving slowly. After another 30 minutes the kudu had migrated into the open. At about 250 yards, nothing was between us and them except for air, grass, and three stands of barbed wire. Periodically, a cow or bull would walk up to the fence, look at it, then turn and walk away. I looked back at Steven and asked again, "Will they jump the fence?" He smiled and nodded. I had my doubts.

Finally, about an hour before dark, two cows jumped the fence directly in front of us. In fact, the biggest bull had been pushing those cows and we whispered that it was time. Expecting the bull to follow, I readied behind my rifle but the bull turned away from the fence. I heard a grunt and looking to my left saw three warthogs headed our way. We all got as flat as possible and they stopped 20 feet to our front.

My body craved movement and finally the warthogs spooked which also spooked the two kudu cows. They turned and jumped the fence, joining back up with the heard. At least now we could breath but it also looked like our opportunity was spoiled. Then another cow jumped the fence and walked right up to us. Geoffrey whispered, "If she gets our scent, we're done." And, she did. The cow whirled in place, ran back to the fence, and jumped it.

We had been prone for about two hours and everything on me hurt. There were thorns poking places you never want a thorn poking. I was almost ready to throw in the towel. I rolled to my side, looked back at Steven and asked, yet again, "Will they jump the fence?" And again, he just grinned and nodded. At least he was consistent.

Geoffrey conceded we only had about 20 minutes of legal shooting light left but an overcast sky was working against our ability to stretch legality to the last minute. Visibility was waning. I dug deep, recommitted, and continued to watch the biggest bull through my binoculars.

I looked at the bull's battleship grey coat and could see the thin and delicate white stripes which worked as camouflage to conceal him in the thick cover. I looked at his high, spiraling horns with ivory white tips that reached toward the darkening heavens. I became mesmerized with his majesty as he slipped through the shadows. I felt like Hemingway, Ruark, and Capstick. I was hunting free ranging kudu in Africa. And then, and then I saw the fence again.

I yelled in a whisper, "Geoffrey! The big guy is at the fence. He's going to jump!" The bull had moved to our left and was almost 300 yards away. I lurched up. My knees and back were screaming in agony but I got into a seated position and looped up in sling.

Kudu were everywhere now, all following the big bull. Looking through the riflescope I was unsure which bull was which. I told Geoffrey to get behind me and to look through his binoculars and confirm – by looking over my rifle – that I was indeed pointed at the biggest one. We were at the very edge of possible and legal shooting light.

"Yes!" Geoffrey said. "You're on him."

That was all I needed to hear. The bright tritium illuminated triangle reticle was already positioned over the bull's vitals. The rifle roared and we were rewarded with the smack of the 150-grain AccuBond. Geoffrey smacked me hard on the back and exclaimed, "We did it. He's down."

I turned and looked at Steven and said, "You were right. They jumped it."

"Yes." He said, smiling, like there was never a question.

I finally had my free-range kudu but I also had the realization that in our modern world, no matter how hard you try, it's almost impossible to hunt without consideration of a fence. High or low, real or imagined, fences are part of hunting. Sometimes those fences are for keeping game in, sometimes for keeping poachers out, and sometimes; sometimes they're there just to make the hunt a little more interesting.

I also learned that when in Africa, trust your tracker. Even if he is a man of few words.

The rifle is a New Ultra Light Arms chambered for the .30 Remington AR. With the 1-4X Trijicon scope it weighs five pounds, 14 ounces.

5 - HARMONY CRONIN - ELK SKINNER

The Madison River joins with the Jefferson and Gallatin at Three Forks, Montana, where the water continues on to the Missouri. The Madison uncharacteristically flows north through the Madison Valley between the Tobacco Root Mountains and the Gravelly Range. Nestled in that valley is a little town called Ennis, which was established at about the end of the Civil War. The current population is around 850 and I think I found that river town's most interesting resident.

Getting 250 pounds of elk meat from Montana to West Virginia requires the assistance of a meat processor/packer. Sure, you could load up multiple coolers and put them on your airplane but there's no guarantee your protein will land at the same airport you do. My hunting partners and I rode into town with my elk and headed straight to Deemo's Meats, the local butcher shop. That's where I met Harmony Cronin.

Elk and deer carcasses were piled waist deep around the receiving door at Deemo's. The mercury was doing all it could to climb to 10 degrees and in the middle of all that frigidness was a blood covered, knife-wielding woman, commanding the operation. I watched her single-handedly drag an elk carcass to her workstation, hook it to a hoist, and proceed to peel off the hide as gracefully as an exotic dancer would slide out of a corset.

Harmony Cronin was originally from Denver and after some wandering settled in Ennis. During those travels she found herself sharing a house with some rats. She set a trap line, caught one, and killed it. That changed everything for Harmony. Dramatically impacted by the experience, she skinned the rat, ate it, and tanned its hide. She become obsessed with the process of using and repurposing animal parts and began to skin and tan every critter she could find. For Harmony, road kill was free entertainment.

While living out of the back of her truck in Ennis, Harmony was tanning hides and making leather goods to sale to tourists traveling to and from Yellowstone. One night at a local saloon she managed to secure an elk hide from a visiting hunter. While taking advantage of his inebriation she found herself at Deemo's Meats and landed a job as an elk skinner. Part of her compensation are elk hides at a discount and elk brains she can use for tanning.

Harmony likes to tan her hides the old fashion way and much of her sewing is done with bone needles. She can professionally skin an elk in about 45 minutes and generally does this about four to six times each day. By the end of season Harmony will have pulled the hide off of more than 250 elk and about half that many deer.

We talked for about 30 minutes and with the elk she was working on stashed in the freezer, she hooked an already skinned Montana whitetail to the hoist and reached for a propane torch. One match later and Harmony was coursing the hide with the flame. Perplexed, I asked her what in the hell she was doing.

She put down the torch, pulled out her knife, and went to work on the front leg, "Getting rid of the hair. I don't have the time to pick off all the hair a hunter who does not know how to skin leaves on his carcass. When the flame hits the hairs they evaporate." And then, like she had done it a thousand times, Harmony put the buck's front leg in an arm bar and broke it with a snap. A disturbing smile crossed her face and she said, "I love that sound." As cool as that was, coming from a girl who's been growing her hair and skinning dead things for eight years, it kind of made my knees hurt.

If you're ever traveling through western Montana, take the time to drive through the beautiful Madison Valley and visit Ennis. Its about 152 miles north of Idaho Falls, ID, and about 52 miles southwest of Bozeman, MT. Hunters should check out the Jumping Horse Ranch and enquire about their combination elk and deer hunts. They are an incredible bargain and they have some of the best whitetail hunting you'll find anywhere. If you're a knee-deep fisherman kind of guy, go by The Tackle Shop and ask for John Way. He's Orvis endorsed and can get you the gear and get you in the water too.

But life is really about people and if you really want to see and talk to someone who's extraordinarily unique and mind-bogglingly talented with a blade, go by Deemo's Meats and ask for Harmony.

Go sober, she has a way with intoxicated hunters.

6 - BORROWED BOOTS

I am not a superstitious person. Black cats crossing my path do not instill panic, I cannot remember a time when I threw salt over my shoulder, and I do not have a lucky hunting hat. I would like to have a lucky hunting hat but I don't even believe in luck.

Don't get me wrong, on occasion when observing a fellow's seemingly effortless success I will marvel at how fortune has found him. And, not too long ago, I managed to put my tag on a nice Montana black bear. That hunt played out in a fashion that would have made a good commercial for a company selling bottled luck or snake oil. Maybe somewhat arrogantly, I do like to attribute good or bad hunts to skill or uncooperative animals.

In October of 2002 I was hunting with Mt. Peyton Outfitters of Bishop's Falls, Newfoundland. Two hours into the first day of a five day hunt, Todd Gillingham - my guide - and I were admiring my first caribou. Boone & Crocket no less! I have told this story many times but it deserves repeating.

My first shot with a .45 caliber muzzleloader took the stag through the liver. He went 100 yards or so and dropped. As we approached to about 15 feet, he came to his feet and plowed right toward us at full throttle. I shoved the muzzleloader forward and, as later described as "luck" by Todd, the bullet broke his spine and he fell at our feet.

I was content to allow that good shooting, not luck, had saved the day and us.

Needless to say when I returned to hunt moose with Mt. Peyton in 2003, I requested to again have Todd as my guide. I was expecting great things. He'd already proved to me he knew what he was doing. Don Tremblett, one of the owners at Mt. Peyton, had extended his hospitality and allowed my sister to come along with the hopes she could take a nice caribou. As expected, I did my best to fill her head with tales of the far north and the hunting adventure awaiting her.

At the same time this hunt was to take place, I had three rifles on loan for test and evaluation. Between us, Sis and I had three tags: caribou for her and moose and bear for me. It would be a great opportunity to add an in the field look at these rifles for the upcoming evaluations I would write. Up until the moment I got on the airplane, things could not have gone any better.

Thanks to the combined efforts of United Airlines and Air Canada, none of my luggage was with me when I presented myself to Canadian Customs. "Most all delayed luggage is delivered to the passenger within 24 hours. It may even make your final destination before you do." Those were the words of the seemingly accommodating and capable baggage guy Air Canada was paying to comfort travelers separated from over $ 6000.00 worth of stuff. He convinced me so I got on my next plane in Toronto and we continued on. Sis, on the other hand, had her rifle and all her other gear on hand for inspection by the Canadian government.

Except for the boots, I will spare you the details of the non-hunting related events of the next three days. I won't tell you about the panic I went into when on the second day Air Canada told me they did not know where my rifles were. I won't go into the anxiety I wallowed through as I saw my struggling outdoor writing career crumble while I tried to conjure ways to tell HS Precision and Kimber that their rifles were gone.

What I will tell you is that all my gear arrived on Wednesday evening and even though the rifle case looked as though it had spent the last three days in a cage with a bi-polar gorilla, both rifles were still sighted in. And, I will offer some advice: Always include extra underwear in your carry-on bag.

Good friend and Mt. Peyton co-owner, Tony Stone, who is also the cook, greeted me at breakfast the first morning with a story about his bad luck with a bull moose on the previous Friday. After two weeks of hard hunting, Tony had managed to make what seemed like a good shot on a bull, with his bow, at about 20 yards. Countless hours of searching had produced no moose. Tony was understandably disappointed. Not just because he had no trophy, but becasue he had wounded an animal. As I relayed my grief of lost luggage I could see Tony's eyes light up. He would now have something to ride me about until my chattels arrived.

As it turned out the weather was as uncooperative as the airlines. Day one was projected to be in the high 80s so there was no need for the cold weather clothes I had packed. Aside from a change of underwear, socks and a pair of boots I would be able to slide by and if a moose or bear presented itself, I could use the Browning BLR in 358 Winchester my sister was carrying. Tony offered me his hunting boots and, believe it or not, they fit perfectly! What are the chances of that happening? Tony also loaned me a light camo jacket and with the exception of the hair on my face, my outward appearance did not change for the next three days.

For those three days I wore Tony's moose hunting - loosing - boots. I walked up and down hills, through wet cement like bogs and over rock after rock. The boots were comfortable to the point that after the second day I offered to buy them from Tony. I did not have the first sign of a blister or discomfort and was not looking forward to giving them back. But nothing lasts forever and on Thursday morning, outfitted in my own stuff, I looked for all-the-world like a professional. I was still wearing Tony's boots; they were just too confortable to give up.

As you would expect, the animals were not moving much at all in the heat except right at dawn and dusk. Todd worked hard and managed to show us several moose. On Wednesday evening Sis used the BLR to take a respectable stag. With her tag filled and me well armed and in fresh underwear, Thursday and Friday were dedicated to finding a bull moose.

And that is where the story comes to the part about coincidence and luck. Friday morning, a week after Tony's disheartening archery adventure with a bull, Todd and I were slowly moving along a narrow timber road when a bull barked just 100 yards or so ahead. We eased into the cover of some alders and Todd gave a quite cow call. Moments later we caught a glimpse of a bull crossing the road to the south. Then, there was a cow and finally Todd said, "There's another one. It's a bull but I cannot tell how big."

The bull was feeding along the edge of the rocky trail framed by alders and fir so thick a weasel would have to follow a beaver to get through it. I eased out of the cover for a better look and saw antler tips, four at first. I signaled to Todd that it was a four point and continued to watch through the riflescope. Then the bull, which had been standing with his used food ejection port facing us, started to turn quartering away. Doing so he raised his head and I saw more antlers…a lot more antlers.

Perfect! I lined the reticle so I was centered on the off-side shoulder and after the slightest touch, the Kimber sent a 200-grain Grand Slam bullet on its way. It smacked the moose with a sound like a Volkswagen hitting an elephant and the bull bolted across the little rocky road. Looking for all the world like a big draft horse that had just been slapped on the ass.

As we were looking for signs of the hit at the point of impact, we heard a grunt. I stepped up on a little berm on the south side of the path and Todd called. When Todd and I hunt together there must be some aroma or aura that encourages big critters to come our way in a hurry because immediately after Todd's call the bull came out of the wall of green right toward us.

I saw antlers and the bull saw me. With amazing agility he turned and headed away as I sent another bullet into him at only about 40 yards. Then all was still.

We circled to another rocky trail that the bull would have to have crossed if he made it out of the 300-foot wide strip of thicket. We found blood and followed it for another 200 yards. Then it stopped. We looked and then we looked some more. No bull. There was nothing to do but give up or cry. On the way back to the scene of the crime Todd remarked the bull was a nice and wide four point. "It was more than a four." I replied.

"No." Todd insisted, "I didn't get a good look at his head when you shot the first time but when he come out of the trees straight at us I counted four long points."

I stopped and looked at Todd and with eyes wide said: "Then we have a problem! After I signaled to you that the bull was a four point he turned his head and there were a bunch more points, that's why I decided to take him. But, when he came out of the trees at us and I saw antlers I instantly began looking for a shot. I was past admiring his rack."

Now Todd's eyes were wide as he excitedly proclaimed, "Then you've shot two moose. I'll bet the one we have been tracking was the second, possibly the result of a bad hit as he was running through the trees. I was sure your hit on the first one was good; I'll bet he is dead, back in the thick stuff, just off the road." So we continued to look. The temperature climbed, we sweated, and the laxative I'd taken on day three finally decided to work. After hours of searching...No bull.

Back at the lodge I blamed it all on Tony. After all, when you wear a man's moose loosing boots, what would you expect? I tried again to buy Tony's boots, thinking that having them bronzed or attached to a plaque would keep them away from my feet and his. Tony wouldn't sell, he doesn't believe in luck either. I'm still not superstitious, but I'll hunt in sandals before I borrow another pair of moose loosing boots.

7 - CHASING DAD

The deer hunter rested on a rock with his rifle across his lap. It was the last day of season and any deer was legal. He was hunting a ridge that fed down from a high mountain. Closer to the top than the bottom, he could see below him well. To his right and left the ridge dropped into deep hollows. Clumps of head high mountain laurel dotted the landscape. The temperature was cool but comfortable and the hunter was wonderfully content, alone on the mountainside.

He was a long way from camp and farther from home. His wife, who usually accompanied him, was at home pregnant with their soon to be first born. After 12 years it looked as though he would now become a father. Munching on an apple his thoughts drifted. He was anxious, about deer he may see and the son he may soon have.

As dusk approached the hunter heard something off to his left. Several deer were moving down the ridge just over the break. Finally, he managed to make out the body of one of the larger deer as it browsed among the thick tangle. With the deer at about 60 yards he shouldered his rifle and squeezed the trigger. At the shot the deer disappeared and he called a miss. In an instant there was another deer, a wide racked buck, coming his way. Under the premise his first shot had gone wide, he worked the pump on his rifle ejecting the empty. That's when the rifle's magazine fell to the ground.

The big buck slid to a stop some 30 feet away and watched the hunter desperately trying to ready his rifle.

More movement distracted the hunter and his attention was drawn back to the spot where he had fired at the first deer. There, another buck with a nice rack was trying to gain his feet. The hunter's first shot had been true, breaking the deer's back. The remaining buck bounded away as the hunter stood, satisfied that he now had venison for his freezer and horns for his wall.

The hunter that day was my father and the deer he took was a 10-pointer with mirror image left and right antlers. Not a trophy book deer but one that would hold the title as being the best buck to come off our hunting property for 35 years. Over those 35 years more than 50 different hunters searched that same property for a buck that would un-throne my father's deer. I chased after that dream too. At first by my fathers side; where he taught me how to hunt, how to slip along quiet like, and how to find the deer. Later, I chased that bigger buck on my own. I hunted hard.

When I was 17 I had my first chance. I was still-hunting an old timber trail on opening day. Gun at the ready, I eased along; one step, stop and look, one step, stop and look. I was checking every bit of the forest for any sign of deer. Another hunter appeared. He was doing the same, headed toward me on the old logging road. When we met we exchanged greetings and passed. Confident the other hunter had spooked any deer in sight of the road, I slung my rifle and started on his backtrack.

I hadn't gone 30 feet when the largest deer I had ever seen stepped into the trail. We were only a handshake apart. Our eyes met and we both knew the other had made a mistake. I struggled to bring the rifle to my shoulder and the buck bolted into the timber, disappearing as quick as he had come.

Strike one.

Two years later found a friend and I as guests at another family's hunting camp. Just at daybreak on opening morning we were all gathered at the back porch talking strategy and readying gear. A field rose away from the little camp and across a high knoll. Feeling a little out of place in the family conversation, I eased over to the fence and started watching the sky turn orange. It was deer time and there, silhouetted on the ridge at about 200 yards, was a wonderfully nice buck. His rack was easily seen without the aid of binoculars. I dropped to a prone position as I alerted the other hunters to my find. One of the family members quickly yelled, "I got him, I got him!"

So, there I lay with my sights on this monster buck's back waiting for the landowner - who was so graciously allowing me to hunt his farm - to shoot and hopefully miss this wonderful buck. The hunter fumbled with his rifle for what seemed like an eternity as the monarch walked into the woods.

Strike two.

It was a long time after that before I got another chance at a deer that might equal my fathers. Sure, I put deer on the meat pole but they were nowhere near Dad's deer. The funny thing about his deer, each year it seemed to demand even more respect. I was still chasing.

Shortly after I had gotten out of the service my folks had bought a small farm that was absolutely littered with deer. Home just before opening day I was without a rifle so I borrowed Dad's. I was working nights at the time and did not get into the woods until around noon. My hopes were that other hunters, coming out for lunch, might get the deer moving. As I entered the timber in a deep hollow at the edge of a field, I saw a heavy racked buck running down the ridge toward open ground. Another chance!

When the buck entered the field I applied what I calculated to be the proper lead and fired all 5 rounds from Dad's rifle.

The buck disappeared over a little rise in the field and I was in shock I had not connected. I quickly slammed a fresh magazine into the rifle and sprinted to the top of the rise. And there, standing proudly about 150 yards away across a draw in the field, was the buck. With a rack much wider than his ears I knew he was the one. After the next five shots the buck slowly walked into the tree line, with me, out of breath and out of ammunition.

"Did you hold a fine bead?" Dad asked.

"No." I mumbled.

Strike three.

The 2000 hunting season found me back at our old hunting camp. On the same ground the now almost mythical 10-point my father had taken 35 years before had come from. A much-improved hunter, I had taken the love of the outdoors and the skills my father had shared with me and built on them. I knew how to hunt deer. Dad doesn't get out quite as far as he used to. Bad knees and an obligation to stay close to take care of Mom, should she need something or should he think she does, keeps him and his rifle near camp. We had worked together that summer to build him a stand in earshot of the cabin.

It was the day after Thanksgiving. I left Dad at his stand and eased up to the top of the mountain. It was a cold 13 degrees when I slipped into the area I had been scouting. In September of that year, just below where I was, I had found a 13-inch strip of velvet at the base of a battered laurel bush. I knew he was there and I was in his bedroom before daylight.

Just as the sun cracked the darkness, with its golden rays breathing life into the colorless forest floor, it happened. A doe burst from other side of the hill onto the big flat I was watching. Right behind her, nose down and in a strut, was the buck. She darted among the wind blown oaks on the hilltop flat with the buck in tow. I had to make a move before she led him away.

I found an opening and fired. He was hit. The buck spun and come toward me and when he stopped broadside at 60 yards I put the second bullet through both shoulders. He wheeled toward me again, head down and coming fast. At 23 steps the rifle roared for the third time and he fell. Three shots, three hits: one for every missed opportunity over the years.

I desperately wanted to drag the big 12-point into camp by myself but even downhill it was too much weight. As bad as I hated it, I left him on the hillside and walked to Dad's stand at the bottom of the mountain.

"That you doing all that shooting up there?" Dad asked.

"Yep." Trying to stay calm I held out a shaking but bloody hand.

"After the second shot I figured you'd missed. Is he a nice one?" Dad was smiling.

"He's the bull of the woods Dad." I was smiling too; I thought the chase was over.

That evening, around the campfire under the stars of Orion, I watched my father as the flames danced between us. I thought about how he had put up with my rowdiness in the woods and other places. It was appropriate he had been there to help bring out the deer that would finally eclipse the one he had brought out 35 years ago. It added to the fond memories while at his side during the many hunts he was never to busy or selfish to take me on.

It was then that I realized that this trail my father had blazed for me to chase him down was much more than just a quest for a bigger buck. It was a road he had built to help me become a hunter. And my chase, I now realized, was far from over. For I had a young son too.

It's not the 10-point buck anymore; it never really was about that at all. It's the obligation to instill the spirit of the hunt in my son like my father did with me. He must be provided with goals to peruse and he must be taught by the good example I must set. I have the obligation to lay the footprints for him to follow while he chases the wide antlered dream just as I did.

The gift must be passed on.

I must make my son a hunter too.

Dad, I'm still chasing you.

8 - CONFESSIONS OF A COONHUNTER

Coonhunters are different. Traveling cornfields and creek bottoms with hounds and headlamps is behavior that would seem strange to some. A lifetime of coonhunting has required me to check my sanity on several occasions. But any look at the adventure and enjoyment gained from those nighttime treks rests my mind that I have not lost it. I was maybe the only kid in my first grade class who could tell coonhunting stories from personal experience. I was fortunate that both of my parents loved to hunt, loved the hounds they did it with, and allowed my juvenile participation. Beyond their love and encouragement that may well be the best gift they ever gave me.

Coonhunting creates a unique set of circumstances other hunting pursuits just don't allow. I've been lost in the dark with no light. I've wrestled a skunk away from a young coonhound pup. I've seen as many as five or six full-grown dogs afraid to take hold of a little ten-pound coon. I've been chased by weasels, fell over cliffs, fell out of trees, seen dogs climb trees and seen them fall out. I've seen dogs bit by snakes, hunters bit by dogs and I've seen hunters get down on all fours and bark up a tree to trying to excite young pups.

Here is a collection of some entertaining events I have been lucky or unlucky enough to bear witness to. To those who have spent many years

on the trail of the ring-tailed bandit you may have had similar experiences and if you don't find these entertaining, hopefully they will jog a memory from your coonhunting past. To the uninitiated or those new to the sport, these tales are merely a taste of the adventure that can await you. Whether unique or
ridiculous, these stories are true and are some of the campfire tales I get to recall and enjoy every fall. These are the confessions of a coonhunter.

Sunday Hunting

Coonhunting has always been a passion with most of my family. Trips to our camp in hunting season found us in the woods every night with our hounds. Sunday hunting in West Virginia was forbidden back then but on one particular night we all decided we were going anyway. At the time we never considered the fact that it was actually Monday morning after midnight. By the time we got into the woods hunting *was* legal.

Along about 2 AM all ten or so of us were relaxing on an old logging road, listening for the dogs to strike up a good trail. Talking and telling stories of hunts past, we never heard the truck coming. Just before it topped the little rise we were all resting on, we saw its lights. Thinking we were illegally in the woods and fearing it was the game warden, we hit the bushes. The truck just so happened to stop right at the spot where we had been resting. The men in the truck, as it turned out, were spot lighting – trying to take a deer illegally. We heard the discussion of their success just down the road.

One of our group had not been able to get completely hidden before the truck pulled up; his feet were sticking out in the road. "Daddy, whose feet are those over there?" Came a voice from the truck.

We heard the truck slam into gear and it tore off down the road so fast we were all sure it was going to wreck. Apparently, they thought *we* were the game warden.

Tough Coons and Mean Opposums

Raccoons have a reputation for being tough and tenacious. An old coon, when put to the ground amoungst several dogs, will roll over on his back and dare anyone or anything to come at him. From that position he has four feet ready to strike and his head can cover 360 degrees in search of any assailant. It's not uncommon for it to be more than the hounds can handle, requiring a follow-up shot by the hunters.

One particular night we had managed to take a large bore coon. He was shoved in my father's hunting vest and the hounds were turned loose in search of another chase. Not too far from the tree, as we were walking through a big field, my father began to dance a little jig while attempting to come out of the hunting vest he was carrying. When the vest hit the ground all was still for a moment as we stared at him and his discarded clothing. A mound rose up in the center of the vest and the old coon just walked out and then ran down through the field. With the dogs gone and the gun unloaded, the bandit escaped.

Treeing or denning a opossum is generally looked upon with displeasure by coonhunters. It never really bothered us a great deal; a chase that ended with a tree or a den was still good music. On one occasion we denned a huge opossum and on arrival at the den we were all shocked to see the opossum's big head sticking out of the hole. We were even more surprised to see him willing to mix it up with the dogs. I had the grand idea that a opossum with a little fight in him would be good for some young pups we had so they could chase him up a tree. We all agreed, and since we were not far from camp, my old army buddy reached down and grabbed the toothy critter behind the head.

We sprinted to the little S-10 Blazer we were hunting out of and Tim and the opossum jumped in the back. We shut the gate and window and tore up the old road to the camp. About a half mile from camp Tim said it looked like the opossum had had enough of the ride. He thought we ought to let him out. Pushing on we made it about another 200 yards when the darnedest bunch of squalling and squealing you've heard broke out in the back of the little SUV. The opossum had decided enough was enough and broke Tim's grip. Not wanting to let the opossum out this far from the camp, my lifelong hunting partner speeded up and we pressed on.

By the time we reached camp Tim had managed to get up on my lap. We bailed out of the truck and turned the pups loose. When we let the tailgate down the opossum jumped off, curled up in a little ball and played dead. The pups had no interest.

Tree Stories

One of the places a great deal of the excitement in coonhunting arises is at the tree. For most, by the time they arrive there the adrenalin rush is peaking. The dogs are praised and the skyward search for the ring-tailed bandit begins. Early season leafs offer concealment for the coon, sometimes making them near impossible to locate.

The use of a coon squealer is common. Shotguns are an alternative. A blast or two of number 6 shot will provide some defoliation. And, if you happen to connect most coons will give you a look, allowing you to spot their glowing eyes.

On one such occasion the hounds put up on a tree in a rainy drizzle. For a good while we searched the leafy top for the coon. It was decided to fire several rounds into the top of the tree with a 410 shotgun in hopes we could make the coon give us a look. The shots were fired and still there were no eyes looking back. The drizzle continued as we led the dogs away and lay under the tree to wait the critter out. In ten or fifteen minutes the rain stopped and one of the hunters asked if we would check his face. "Something is wrong with my face, it's a drawing up on me!" He exclaimed. "I might be having a stroke!"

We all rushed to see what could be troubling the hunter and found his face covered in dried blood. A pellet or two had actually struck the old coon and the hunter had laid down right under him. Thinking the moisture on his face was the rain, he paid no attention to it. But, as it dried, he became concerned he was under the grip of a terrible circumstance.

As I said, excitement runs high at the tree and not just for the hunters. The dogs are anxious to get a little fur in their mouth and are often in a frenzy. Once, while hunting several young pups, we managed to tree a coon up a small locust tree on a steep hillside. We decided to try to put the coon out to the pups and hold the old dogs while the youngsters had a little fun.

My longtime hunting partner was always in search of a better coon shooter and had decided a .22 pistol was just the trick. It would be easy to carry all night and was plenty of gun to pop a raccoon out of a tree. My old dog was a very powerful hound and for lack of a better place to tie him, I slipped my foot through the loop in the lead. After about a half box of shells I had managed to totally excite all the dogs, wihtout hitting the coon.

With each shot they thought the coon would come tumbling down.

The fact that the coon was only about 20 feet up and visible to the hounds only added to their frenzy.

At last I managed to connect and the coon fell to the ground. Rocket, my old dog, shot down the hill toward the fight that had ensued on the ground. he seemed not to mind at all that he had jerked me from my feet and was dragging me down the hill with him. All while I was trying to keep the loaded .22 pistol in a safe direction as I fumbled with the safety. Four dogs, a man with a pistol, and a somewhat disgruntled coon in a pile was a quite comical sight but not a pile I could recommend being in.

Worthless Dogs

My first coon dog was no coon dog at all. Oh, he would run and tree sometimes if another dog would help him. That is when he wasn't chasing a deer or a fox. His worst trait was that he was mean at the tree or around any other dog. I never knew why. I always treated him well and was proud of him because, if for no other reason, he was mine. It got to the point we could not hunt him because of his disposition. My grandfather said the dog needed put down. I suggested giving him to another hunter.

"Another hunter won't be as tolerant as you and may be mean to him. He's good for nothing on his own and you can't hunt him with other dogs." Grandfather was right. I had seen hunters get rough with their dogs and didn't want it to happen to old Nate.

That was a tall order for a 12-year-old boy and a 38 Special. I learned a hard lesson about the finality of death and the responsibility of adulthood. Although there was no suffering for Nate, I shed my tears when no one else was looking. It may seem cruel to some but not as cruel as it can be for a pet or hunting dog nobody wants.

My Grandfather has been gone for many years now. I like to think he is somewhere taking care of Nate and other hounds of coonhunting past.

Work and family has separated me from nighttime excursions. I still get to hunt, its just other game and during normal business hours. On occasion I will step out back at our old hunting camp and in the darkness I will hear a lonesome bawl of a hound echo off the mountain.

It always stirs the same memory. One of lying in a high meadow with grandfather and my cousin who has became my best friend. As we would stare into the heavens, listening to our dogs work a cold track in the hollow below, Grandpa would say, "Wonder what the poor folk are doing?"

Of course financially, we were just as poor as anyone. But, right then, right there, we were as rich as could possibly be.

Circa 1975: Dad with Bonnie Blue, a rattlesnake cur and maybe the best coonhound that ever lived.

9 - WALT BERGER - BULLETSMITH

Back in 2006, before folks realized Berger's VLD bullets were suitable for hunting, Walt Berger gave me a tour of the Berger Bullets' factory. A few days later we flew to New Zealand to hunt. During those 10 days Walt told me his story.

Walt's story is legendary, but it's not one of fighting demons or overcoming all odds. Rather, it's the story of a shooter's quest for perfection, the story of a hunter crossing new mountains, and, it's the story of a man realizing the American dream.

Growing up Outside

Walt was born in Easton, Ohio, in 1928. He was one year old when the stock market crashed. Times were tough, but when he was five he scrounged up a BB gun and like Roosevelt, it promised a "New Deal." Walt's dad liked to hunt. He enjoyed chasing raccoons, rabbits, and fox with scent hounds. It's a pursuit as infectious as Ebola. I know; I grew up with a father who had the same passion.

The outdoors became Walt's playground. He was a product of The Depression, a time when you made your own way, created your own entertainment, or lived an unhappy existence. Walt's way was found in the wild, and he funded his adventures by selling coon hides and collecting a 25-cent bounty on groundhogs he shot with an Iver Johnson .22. So passionate was Walt about hunting that he and a friend rode, with their .22 rifles, from Easton, Ohio to Fort Knox, Kentucky, in the *trunk* of a friend's 39 Plymouth, just so they could squirrel hunt.

And then, there was another crash. War took Walt's brother and best friend away to fly B-17s and assault beaches. Walt, too young to go, stayed at home and continued to hunt. Walt coon hunted with his .22 rifle and a lantern. He'd blow out the lantern when trespassing. One night, while crossing property he did not have permission to hunt, the owners saw his lantern from their house. They started shooting and Walt hastily blew out his lantern and got behind a tree. Walt told me, "I remember thinking, my brother is off in the war and I'm at home hunting his dog, and damned if I ain't the one going to get shot. I learned then and there that sometimes being in the dark could be a good thing!"

Walt eventually registered for the draft but was never called. A high school basketball and baseball player, and a track star, Walt most likely had a 1A rating with no exemptions. Walt later learned that no one in his home county who registered during the month of November 1946 got called up. The courthouse lost all the draft registrations from that month.

Bullet Failure

Out of school, he went to work for a box factory. With the promise of a supervisory potion, he decided to pass on college. In 1949 Walt became a husband and, inspired by the writings of Jack O'Connor, bought a life insurance policy to later finance a sheep hunt. At a gun shop in Akron, he also bought his first centerfire rifle for $198. It was a Winchester Model 70 Featherweight in .257 Roberts.

Walt and a friend practiced religiously in preparation for a hunt in Pennsylvania, even shooting a target inside a tire they rolled down the hill.

On the first day of the hunt Walt jumped a buck and he shot it as it ran off. It disappeared and another hunter shot at it. After a short argument, Walt walked away from the second deer he had lost to a bullet that failed him. The first was a whitetail he dropped with a 16-gauge slug a few years before. When Walt walked up to that deer and pulled out his trench knife it got up and ran away. The deer crossed a ridge and there was another shot and another argument about whom the deer belonged to. Walt had lost that argument too.

Bench Rest Shooting

A few years later, while returning from a western hunt with some friends, their car broke down near Buffalo, Wyoming. In the process of getting it fixed they learned about a benchrest shooting match near town. They fixed the car, stopped by the range, and Walt saw his future.

At Walt's first benchrest match he didn't have enough cash to meet the entry fee so they let him compete, ineligible for prize money. It was there he learned that to be competitive he would have to make his own bullets. So, he took a second job carrying blocks and cement to pay for the dies. Two-hundred-and-seventy-five dollars later he owned a set of .224 bullet dies, which enabled him to win a few matches. He even sold a few bullets. Walt continued to perfect his bullet-making skills. This required lots of testing and the investment of a substantial amount of cash, just so he could shoot smaller groups. It wasn't long until Walt earned a reputation, and fellow competitors were not happy when Walt and his bullets showed up.

In 1963 Spiveco Inc. began making the J4 bullet jacket; these were bullet jackets with a total indicated run-out (TIR) of 3/10,000 or less at the base and 5/10,000 or less at the mouth. The jackets changed the landscape as far as benchrest shooting was concerned, and Walt and almost everyone else began using them. Walt continued to shoot with perfection and win awards. He became a Bench Rest Hall of Fame member, and he cashed in his insurance policy and went on that sheep hunt. And, in 1989, Berger Bullets, a garage operation, became Walt's full-time job.

The VLD

In 1985 Louis Palmisano, one of the originators of the .22 PPC cartridge, approached Walt about making a new, game-changing bullet called the VLD (Very Low Drag.) The major difference in the VLD was its incorporation of a secant as opposed to the common tangent ogive and the inclusion of a long, 90-degree boat-tail. This high-caliber secant ogive and steep angle boat-tail drastically increased the ballistic coefficient of the bullet, which gave it a flatter trajectory and better wind resistance.

Walt agreed, and his bullet-building success continued. But, unlike many who dream of turning a passion into a profitable business, Walt did not go out and borrow money to fund his company. Up until 1997, everything Walt had ever purchased, he'd paid for with cash. In the process he instilled in his kids and grandchildren the concept of saving to buy what you want instead of borrowing. Walt told me how he learned about taking care of money, "When I was still young I once hid some money under a bridge in a mason jar. A flood came and I lost it all. It was about $14. After that, I was always careful what I did with my money."

Match Bullet or Hunting Bullet

Berger Bullets did not go in debt until 1997 when the company purchased a bullet-making machine. They had to do it to meet demand. Prior to 1997, every Berger bullet was made by hand. Berger Bullets became, and remains to this day, the premier manufacturer of match-grade bullets, which still use J4 jackets. In fact, at the turn of the century, Berger Bullets merged with Spiveco and became the sole manufacture of J4 jackets.

Surprisingly, through customer feedback, Walt learned his VLD bullets were also amazingly effective on big-game animals. Their lethality is a combination of how their construction delays expansion until the bullet is at vital-organ depth. Combine this with their almost grenade-like eruptive deformation and the flat trajectories possible with the high ballistic coefficients of the VLD design, and you have a premium big game bullet like no other.

The One That Didn't Get Away

On a cloudy New Zealand day in early 2007 Walt Berger–the hunter–would take another .257 Roberts and put down a red stag, with one shot, using a 115-grain Berger VLD bullet. The stag did not get up and run away. Like millions of times before, Walt Berger calculated the proper hold, placed the reticle in the right spot, controlled his breathing, and pulled the trigger with the same precision and attention to detail that has guided his entire shooting and bullet-making career. This time there was no question, no argument, and no confusion about who shot the animal. And, there was no question who built the bullet or if it had worked.

Walt Berger was the driving force behind the organization of the first World Benchrest Shooting Match. He developed a standard for the manufacture of bullets now revered by bulletsmiths worldwide. He distinguished himself as a world-class bench rest shooter, and he has set an example of leadership and character for his family, friends, and associates to follow.

Some shooters think of Walt Berger when they seat a streamlined, precision-engineered bullet into a brass case. Some think about him when they see that single hole made in a target by ten successive shots. And, others think of him every time they see a rifle thrown over some sandbags. When I think of Walt Berger, I think about a young boy like me, following coonhounds and stalking groundhogs with a .22 rifle. I think of a man, like my father, who through hard work, dedication, and a relentless quest for perfection managed to make the most out of the American dream. And I think of the irony of how his motivation to build the best match bullet ever also produced one of the deadliest hunting bullets of all time.

10 - THE PROBLEM WITH ELAND

With his rifle braced over shooting sticks and dusk approaching, Charlie placed the bold reticle in the Kahles scope on the center of the bull eland's chest. At the shot, the bull reacted as though hard-hit. Hennie Badenhorst, a professional hunter who has witnessed countless African game animals take bullets, gave Charlie a congratulatory slap on the back and announced, "Good shot!" Both men were smiling as they walked across the bushveld south of the Limpopo River.

The corners of their mouths dropped with their spirits when they arrived at the spot where the eland had been standing. No blood. Darkness was fast consuming the South African sky, so Hennie suggested they unleash the track dogs. Confident the bull was hit solidly, they both expected the track to be short. It was.

In moments, the three hounds were at bay. Charlie and Hennie ran to the scene and found the dogs circling an eland cow that was down with a broken rear leg. At Hennie's direction, Charlie finished the cow off with a head shot from his 9.3mm rifle and Hennie proclaimed the hunt as over.

Like a kid who lost his first tee-ball game, Charlie approached the campfire that evening with his head low. At the fire, he told of the stalk, the shot, the dogs, and how Hennie had concluded that the 286-grain Nosler Partition had only superficially wounded the bull, fragmented, continued on, entered the cow low in the chest, and came out, breaking the rear leg. I was skeptical, so we carried the investigation to the skinning pole, where the trackers were peeling the hide from the eland.

Based on the autopsy, I reached a more plausible conclusion. The rear leg was broken, but there was no blood, and the bone was not shattered, as you would typically expect from a bullet wound. On the surface, the chest appeared to have some wounds, but closer examination showed to the satisfaction of Charlie, the skinners, and me, that a bullet was not the cause. These wounds were nothing more than punctures and scrapes suffered by the cow as she stumbled and fell because of the broken leg, which most assuredly had occurred without the aid of Charlie or his Nosler Partition.

Of course, the track dogs had done their job. The herd of eland spooked after Charlie's shot and the dogs took up the track. With no blood evidence the dogs and hunters called it a "find" when they came across the injured cow. This was a reasonable, in the field, conclusion that fell apart under a coroner-style investigation, even without the aid of a forensics expert like Henry Lee. The only bullet the cow eland had received was the finishing shot Charlie put to her head.

Charlie's PH didn't buy our conclusions, nor did he participate in the investigation at the skinning pole. Of course, this was Hennie's court, and we had no jury to deliberate our findings. I won't say that when the time came for Charlie to take his eland, he had "seen the elephant," but he had seen other, nobler animals like the kudu. Charlie Sisk builds custom hunting rifles for a living, and Charlie knows how to shoot those rifles. And, Hennie Badenhorst is a professional hunter of vast and varied experience. Sometimes, experience is just not enough.

Two days prior, Charlie Sisk and I had been bouncing along the two-track in the back of the bakkie when our PH, Pieter Lessing, spotted a brute of a warthog. We bailed out and began a scoot across the bushveldt on Pieter's heels. When Pieter's palm came up, we froze. Seconds later, Pieter turned to me and whispered he had spotted an eland bull bedded 150 yards to our flank. Earlier that morning our hunting companion Pat had wounded an eland. Was this the one? We promptly forgot the warthog.

Guided by hand signals, Charlie and I followed behind Pieter. The bull was bedded under a huge monkey-thorn tree, and after about 20 minutes, we were within cat-kicking distance. We found our own tree and stacked up like a SWAT team behind its massive trunk.

"Let me confirm this is Pat's bull and if it is, put as many bullets in him as you can before he gets gone." Pieter said as his gaze shifted from my eyes to the 6.5mm rifle in my hands. It was the only rifle between the three of us.

Making sure the Kahles Multi-Zero scope was set at its 100 yard zero, I eased around the tree and placed the reticle at the base of the eland's skull, unconcerned the 125-grain Partition would lack enough oomph to stop the bull with a hit where I was aiming. I crouched, motionless, hoping we could end the suffering of a wounded animal and collect Pat's trophy. "I cannot see a wound," Pieter whispered. "I am going to have to make him stand. Be ready if I tell you to shoot."

Pieter barked at the bull, putting him on his feet. Tempted to look for a wound myself, I focused my attention on keeping the reticle at the juncture of the eland's head and neck as he turned. I waited for the command but it never came. This bull was uninjured and the eland Pat wonded was never found.

Earlier that morning, professional hunter Anton Vandernest had gained Pat a position within bow range of an eland bull. Pat's Leupold filled edge to edge with the tawny hide, and after the shot, the only indication the eland had ever existed was a couple of drops of blood and a burning memory. Later, Pat would confess that maybe he ought to have turned the scope's magnification down from 9X at that close range to be more certain of putting the bullet in the stopping place.

We will never know about either of the eland these two hunters lost. Some of the hunters, including me, suspect Charlie's bull did not go far and would likely have been found if the injured cow had not confused the issue. As for Pat's eland, it's a toss-up. The track dogs were not available for assist that day to assist and his PH and native trackers failed the spoor.

Our hunting party's third eland encounter occurred after another hunter and his PH had been working a mature bull for most of the morning. When a clear shot came the result was not what they anticipated. The 260-grain, .375 caliber, Nosler AccuBond traveled lengthwise through the eland and stopped short of exit without hitting anything important. After several hundred yards, the blood trail stopped.

When we arrived with the track dogs, there was a look of concern on the hunter's face. Jan Kleynhans, his PH, felt that the bull was down somewhere close, sick from the bullet through his gut. He was right. The dogs busted the eland out of his bed after going less than 200 yards.

Jan, Hennie, Sisk, and the hunter all rushed ahead through a snarl of thorn and brush that made it impossible to see even an animal as big as an eland until you were on top of it. I had elected to in the bakkie, which was parked along the two-track, out of the way of the dogs and hunters. I heard the shot, and I heard the dogs continuing on. The spectacle was occurring less than 200 yards away but was completely out of sight in the dense vegetation. Having hunted with hounds all my life, I was able to piece the action together by ear.

A pumpkin-thumping thud and a squall signaled the eland had connected with a kick. A second shot told me the hunters were close, but the continued baying of the hounds, moving at a good pace through the brush, told me the eland was still on his feet and still on the move. Moments later, the bull appeared in the road, with the dogs close behind. He was hurt, but his oil light wasn't on. Even with a broken front leg, he was still under power and still putting forth a respectable effort to make a blood puddle out of the dogs.

The situation was dangerous for the dogs and pitiful for the eland. I did not like it. That day I was hunting with a .257 Roberts but Charlie's .338 Win. Mag. was in the Land Rover so I snatched it up and chambered a round. The bull, with the hounds in tow, was headed toward me at about 130 yards. I quickly placed the reticle on the eland's chest, like the knot on a necktie, and the rifle bucked. Like always, I worked the bolt while the rifle was in recoil, but before a new cartridge slammed home, the bull was down and motionless.

The hunter, like Charlie and Pat, could handle a rifle. Just the day before he had made a long, tough shot on an escaping red hartebeest and we had all shared the roasted back straps of a steinbuck he had taken the same day. But maybe, maybe eland are different.

The next day, while Hennie was stalking an impala with another hunter, Charlie and I sat in the high seats of the Land Rover witnessing the makings of a fine African sunset.

"Joe was a bit upset at you for shooting his eland." Charlie is never one to beat around the bush.

"I was upset too." I said.

Charlie's forehead wrinkled as he asked, "Why were you upset?"

"I won't abide an animal suffering needlessly," I said sternly. "I'll end it if I can. Don't care who put the first bullet in it. Wasn't going to let him hurt the dogs, either."

"It put him down like an 88mm on the turret ring of a T-34." Charlie was letting his German heritage show. "You know we were pretty close to the bull when you shot."

"The shot was safe. And necessary," I said. "I'd do it again tomorrow."

A long silence was broken by the call of a go-away bird. "I don't like an animal to suffer either." Charlie finally said. "If I get into a running gun battle with an eland, or anything else, shoot if you can."

Dusting my binoculars with the brush of my lens pen, I looked Charlie in the eye, "I would expect no less from you."

Thru a big Texas grin, Charlie rhetorically asked, "We just can't have any luck with these eland, can we?"

Nodding, I grinned back, "I don't believe in luck and even if I did, sometimes luck just ain't enough."

Eland, What is enough?

Eland are big, the largest of Africa's antelope. In the book The Perfect Shot, Kevin Robertson recommends bullets of at least 200 grains and cartridges along the lines of the 9.3x62mm or .375 H&H, with allowances for smaller cartridges like the .338 Winchester Magnum and .35 Whelen as being suitable.

Of the several PHs I have hunted with before, during, and since the hunt with Charlie Sisk, I've been most impressed by Fort Richmond Safari's Geoffrey Wayland, who is the youngest of the lot. His father taught him to shoot on their ranch south of Kimberly in the Northern Cape and Geoffrey has an uncanny knowledge of animal habits and anatomy.

He doesn't get all that caught up in cartridges because he understands bullets placed properly are what end hunts. I was along with him and another hunter who put an eland down with a .30-06.

Of course, that's the trick with any rifle — put the bullet in the right spot. This may mean that you avoid certain shot opportunities that offer less than ideal angles. It also means a hunter should fight to keep the effects of adrenalin under control and strive to not pull the trigger until he is confident he has reined-in his excitement and can direct the bullet with precision.

The hunter who wounded the eland I shot had a .375 H&H and the AccuBond bullets he was shooting performed as their designer intended. The problem was, they missed the vitals. Charlie Sisk and Pat Cocker both used a wildcat cartridge, designed by Charlie, based on the 8mm Remington Magnum case. It launches a 9.3mm, 286-grain, Nosler Partition at a terrific velocity of 2,775 feet per second. Enough gun, for sure.

The problem with eland is that they are big and magnificent animals. They are also rather expensive and in Africa you pay if you draw blood, regardless if the animal is ever found. This puts some pressure on hunters who have been told how hard they are to kill. The pressure compounds under the watchful eye of a so-called professional and shots often land wide of their mark. I believe hunters often think the eland - not its heart - is the target.

I am not particularly enamored with the eland as a trophy animal. However, I would gladly shoot one again under the promise of seeing pieces of it on my plate. Next to sable, it is without question the best meat I've ever tasted. If that opportunity arises, I will worry more about my shooting than my cartridge or bullet, and I will do my best to put the bullet in the right spot. So far, I've taken three eland with four shots. Like with all big game animals, good shooting tends to be enough.

11 - FALLING DOWN

Make more than just a casual appearance in the outdoors and sooner or later you will fall down. (Real hunters never fall down. They may, on occasion, loose their balance or footing but never, ever, do they fall down.) Men who never worry about their wardrobe or get overly concerned with their outward appearance transform during hunting season. Suddenly, they feel they must venture out in a matched camouflaged ensemble, becoming as
fashion conscious as a starlet headed to the Oscars. And, it seems that hats are as important to the outdoorsmen as those worn by high-class debutants at the Kentucky Derby. All this nonsense makes a fall in the woods akin to Charlize Theron bouncing her noggin off the red carpet.

There are only two accepted ways to fall or deal with a fall in the great outdoors. This is important information to know because you can never be sure that you are alone. Some well hidden camo clad hunter may be present to witness your tumble. This, as you can imagine, could be a potentially embarrassing situation capable of tainting your reputation as a woodsman. I will detail these ways and means here with examples - to insure your continued status as a man of the woods.

The "Get Up Quick" Technique

I was hunting turkey with Kahles Optics in the West Virginia hills. My guide was Larry Case, an outdoorsman of the highest order. All morning Larry had entertained me with outdoor writer horror stories. I was trying to put my best foot forward and not leave a negative impression like some of the other literary icons – or nut jobs - Larry had guided. We were walking an old haul road as smooth and flat as a Wal-Mart parking lot when for some unknown and completely illogical reason, I simply forgot that I was walking and found my nose headed for the ground in a hurry.

Realizing how this display of clumsiness would do little to improve Larry's perception of outdoor writers, let alone me, I knew I had to act quickly. In an effort to thwart becoming another of Larry's outdoor writer campfire tales, I employed the "get up quick" technique, rolled with the fall and sprang back to my feet. Though the exercise was not that smooth, I did keep my nose and reputation out of the mud. This technique can be a status saver when you step on a slick limb hidden under fallen leaves on a steep hillside or when your foot finds a slimy creek rock in a mountain stream.

The " I Believe I Will Sit Here" Ploy

Sometimes, getting up quick is not an option. A fall may put you in a predicament that will leave you sprawled upon the forest floor. A good friend and hunting companion is a master of this modus operandi, not only after a fall but he's equally adapt making almost any mistake - too include a bad shot - shine brightly even when the light seems dim.

Several of us were hunting a rocky ridge with questionable footing for even a mountain goat. My partner, who was negotiating a log, found the law of gravity still applied in Virginia as much as it did in West Virginia and landed hard, rear end first, on the far side of the log. He even lost his hat in the collapse.

(Here's another tip: any time you lose your hat in a fall, wipe you brow and adjust your hair - if you have any - to distract from the uncovering.)

Without losing a breath, my friend extended his arm and pointed down into the hollow. "This is a good place." he said, gesturing to a small thicket of pines a 100 yards down the ridge to his left. "I expect a nice buck might just try to slip by here directly. I believe I will sit here." We eased off and not 20 minutes later heard a shot. Without question it was the grandest display of fall-covering I have ever witnessed.

There is one other useful tactic for dealing with a fall. It only works when your fall is for sure unobserved. Its also very helpful when explaining away any injuries sustained in said fall.

First, before you attend to any wounds, call out for help with just enough volume to alert anyone who may have been close enough to see. Don't scream, it is not to your benefit to attract a hunter from the next hollow over. Then, when you are sure the tumble went un-witnessed, tend your hurts and start devising your "fall" story. Consult the supplied guide to help you properly formulate an explanation for your scrapes, cuts, and bruises.

Remember, temporary loss of vertical positioning is common in the outdoors; it can happen to anyone. The hard part and the thing that sets the professional outdoorsman apart from the tenderfoot, is not only the getting up, but the justification for the fall itself. Best have a strategy worked out before hand and it's not a bad idea to practice the get up quick technique in advance.

Just be sure there's no one watching.

THE GUIDE FOR FALLING DOWN
IN THE OUTDOORS

1. Never admit to falling from a treestand.

2. Shear drop offs and rock cliffs are perfect locations to build a fall story around.

3. Always coincide the moment of your fall with an attempt to get a shot off at a trophy animal.

4. If you are hunting in absolute flat country consider incorporating an effort to fend off a pack of angry coyotes, a herd of rattlesnakes or alien abduction into your fall story.

5. Use the table below to gauge the distance of your fall.

Bruises and small scratches................................No less than six feet.
Wounds that require stitches..At least 10 feet.
Simple fractures............15 feet plus one for foot every broken bone.
Compound fractures / head injuries....................No less than 20 feet.

12 - FIRST LIGHT

The wool collar feels good turned up against your neck and like a submarine you try to sink deeper into the warmth of your jacket. Snowflakes the size of silver dollars drift slowly toward the ground, like goose feathers from a busted pillow. The eastern sky is pastel pink but the color seems so far away. You think if you could reach out and touch the glow it would warm you. All is still. So still you can almost hear the snow as it softly and silently crashes to the ground.

In the distance you hear cows welcoming a farmer to the pasture and you imagine the old man throwing hay bales off the back of his battered Ford. A mile away, on the next ridge ,you see what must be a flashlight moving through the trees as a hunter heads to his stand.

You think to yourself: "He's late."

Closer, an owl breaks the silence. It startles you. You shudder and recognize the cold again. The owl's question of "Whoooo..?" makes you feel he is talking to you. Wanting to know why you are there and what you are doing.

Then, all is still again.

At first you pass off the faint noise as insignificant, a squirrel stirring for breakfast at most. You hold your breath listening. Listening. Nothing. You slowly exhale and the fog seems to hang like a ghost in the crystal cold air. You hear it again. Directly behind you just over the crest of the ridge. The sound is but a faint, brief whisper in the predawn silence.

Is it the buck? It could be a raccoon, going to his den. Or maybe, a last acorn finally letting go.

In the summer you found his tracks, deep and wide, in the hollow where he crosses the stream. During late September he showed you he was heavily antlered when you found the healthy evergreens gouged deep by his brow tines. And last week he showed you his territory, freshly scraped earth saturated with his musky odor. Now, you have intruded into his domain. You know he lives here; the sign does not lie. But will he show? Did you listen when Dad was talking? Teaching? Did you learn?

Your rifle is across your lap. Removing your hands from the warmth of your armpits you grip the old gun. It feels familiar, comfortable, and you pull it close to your body. Your finger finds the safety. The checkering is smooth at the wrist and forearm and you remember the hands of your father that made it that way. You remember how they used to hold the rifle and how you always wanted to. And, you remember how he could be motionless, for what seemed like hours, with the rifle at the ready. Now you embrace it tight across your chest. The smell of oil-impregnated walnut is strong.

You smell Dad.

And you wait.

You hear the sound again, edging ever closer. You tense and touch the safety again. Your pulse quickens. Heart loud in your chest, you breathe deep looking for oxygen to calm the rush and the cold air chills your lungs.

You shiver. Almost uncontrollably.

Light is coming and so is he.

13 - MELVIN FORBES - RIFLE MAGICIAN

The history of the rifle revolves around just a few men. Jacob and Samuel Hawken gave the muzzleloader respect that has remained untarnished for almost 200 years. John Browning applied a level of engineering rapidity, volume, and genius of which has never been matched. And, Paul Mauser concocted a rugged, metallic work of art that, to this day, is spoken of as if it were the Holy Grail.

For those John Barsness calls "rifle loonies," the names of Hawken, Browning, and Mauser are akin to gun god disciples. Admittedly, there are a few others. Richard Gatlin, John Garand, and Hiram Maxim left their mark too, partly because of their ingenuity but very much because their inventions carried their names.

A most revolutionary rifle advancement occurred, almost unnoticed, in the mid 1980s. That's when a machinist, a mold maker, a high school shop teacher, and a part-time gunsmith perfected the bolt-action sporting rifle by applying as much attention and ingenuity to the stock as to the steel. This new rifle was impressively accurate and unbelievably light. Remarkably, the machinist, mold maker, shop teacher, and gunsmith were all the same person. Even more remarkable is the fact that you probably don't know his name.

Why? His friends and associates who invested in his incredible creation insisted the company be named Ultra Light Arms (ULA) now New Ultra Light Arms (NULA). In 1985 the name seemed reasonable because lightweight sporting rifles did not exist. What these investors did not foresee was that these gravity-defying rifles, that also defied conventional wisdom, would start a trend. A plethora of copycat rifles, from manufacturers like Kimber, Remington, Ruger, Winchester, and just about everyone else emerged. And, they were marketed as "ultra lights," thus marginalizing the name of the rifle that started the movement.

Because their name was descriptive of their qualities as opposed to being distinct and proper in nature, the rifles from ULA became lost in a sea of lesser quality, under performing knock-offs. These imitations found success through poor replication of a rifle that created the genre that allowed them to exist at all. But, the inability of mass-produced, light-weight, bolt-action rifles to deliver premium performance diminished the entire concept. What's in a name? Sometimes everything.

True rifle loonies tried these facsimiles because they believed, like Townsend Whelen said, "A man will travel farther, hunt over more country, have a better chance of coming on game, and be in better condition when he does if his weapon is light." After repetitive disappointments these men learned, through the writings of other men like Aagaard, Carmichael, Barsness, and Petzal, the origin of the lightweight bolt-action rifle concept. And, they learned about the man who made it a reality: a West Virginian named Melvin Forbes.

The brilliance of Forbes' design is that a committee of different men with varying areas of expertise did not conceive it; a single man developed it with a committee of different skill sets, which he had learned over his lifetime. Forbes used his experience hunting in the hills of West Virginia to format the heft and ergonomics.

He used his machining brilliance to impeccably craft the steel and his mold making knowledge to create the magical stock. And, he used his shop experience to turn the screws. When he became stumped, he turned to experts, like the aerospace engineers at the Allegheny Ballistics Laboratory.

In the end, his ability to balance his mechanical and hunting background produced a perfectly balanced rifle. A rifle like Whelen could only have dreamed of. When he took his rifle to the range it did things he'd never seen a rifle do. He found that he only had to zero it one time because the combination of the full-length bedding and the unique stock, which was stiffer than the barrel, held zero no matter the weather. He discovered that all loads shot to essentially the same point of impact. And, he realized that precision accuracy was possible without a heavy barrel.

Without a full understanding of the science at work, Forbes walked over to West Virginia University and asked them to conduct comparative tests. That's were he discovered the true magnificence of what he had accomplished. His hand-built, one-pound stock of carbon fiber and Kevlar was actually dampening barrel vibrations. In fact, barrel vibrations were non-existent after 12 inches.

New Ultra Light Arms Model 20 Short.

Yes, Forbes had created a marvelous rifle but the hero was the stock. It was not just a wood or injection molded handle; it was a purpose-built, handcrafted chassis, designed to strengthen and enhance the performance of the steel. It was not there to just give the shooter something to hold on to. The stiffness and straightness of the stock pushed recoil back into the shooter so that it could be better controlled. The shape of the stock had a 20% higher interface with the shooter. And, its one-pound weight allowed for perfect balance to be achieved.

Those who have not experienced a rifle built by Melvin Forbes cannot believe. Their exposure to the rifles designed by men like Browning and Mauser have left them skeptical of what is possible. Their disappointment with chopped down, skeletonized sporting rifles soured their lust for a true, ultra light hunting rifle. Unless they find faith in the words of those who have seen the magic, they are destined to carry a heavy load. They will forever consider a less than six pound .308 Winchester unstable and inaccurate.

Melvin Forbes had cast rifle magic. And, during the last 30 years, he has built a legion of riflemen who, while they might not understand the magic (science) they trust it. As unfathomable as it may seem, three out of four of those who buy a rifle from Melvin Forbes buy another one, often within the next 12 months. I own five.

What Melvin Forbes has been unable to do is wrap all this wonderment up into a package that will fit inside a single paycheck of the average American but, this package does not carry his name. For this reason, and this reason alone, his name will never be as well known as Hawken, Browning, and Mauser. However, for the fortunate few who believe, his name is just as respected and revered.

Melvin Forbes' name belongs on the list of iconic rifle engineers because he realized the rifle stock is just as important as the rifle steel and he was the first and last to make a truly light-weight, accurate, and dependable bolt- action rifle.

Melvin Forbes is a rifle magician and magic – science – is real. If you want to experience it first hand, all you have to do is believe and write a check.

But when you do Melvin will tell you, "That's my rifle, you're just paying to have it on permanent loan."

Rifle magician Melvin Forbes and the prototype rifle he built in 1984.

14 - THE DRAG

The cold air hurts your lungs but you breathe it anyway. A deep breath for every step. Your thighs ache as you again lean into the rope and struggle to pull. Just one more foot. Almost there, almost to the crest of the ridge, you keep telling yourself it will all be down hill from there.

John would have come back with you to help but you weren't going to leave him there. Not alone on the mountainside. It wouldn't be right. You had looked to long, searched, and planned too hard to abandon him. He deserved your effort. He was now your responsibility.

You pulled harder.

He followed.

You go to one knee at the crest. With the electric red at your back and the full moon overhead you look down in the little valley. You can barely make out the smoke climbing from the chimney as it trails off down along the creek. The door to the cabin is open and the glow from the fire illuminates John as he stands leaning against the door jam. You imagine he is holding a hot cup of coffee and wondering why you are late. If you called you think he would come. He is and he would. You stay silent.

You feel a chill. Sitting back on your heels you look down at the buck. His hide is dark but his antlers seem to glow in the moonlight. You reach out and place your still trembling hand on his chest. His hair is soft and he is still warm. It calms you. You press deep and imagine the beating heart you fought so hard to stop.

His spirit was strong and it has given you strength.

You thirst, you hunger, and you yearn for the fireside to warm your body and to tell your story. His protein will nourish your family. His hide will make your moccasins. His memory will keep you young. But there is no rush, that all can wait.

With your hand on the buck, his fur between your fingers, and your heart in your throat, you do the only thing you can. You do what seems right.

Sit alone at his side for just a little bit longer.

15 - HOOK SET DEEP

I don't fish anymore. I gave it up when my oldest son was born. The year before I had purchased a bass boat and in the few weekends I could get it to the lake I managed to almost drown my former brother-in-law and catch one really big carp. I've been once since; I took my son fishing when he was about five. We both got wet and in an argument over how he should hold his pole.

When I was younger I fished a lot. My family had a camp on the New River and as a school board employee my father had the summers off. That's where we spent them. It wasn't much of a camp, just a three room shack with a screened in porch and roll roofing covering the outside walls. It was on a remote section of the river and the only access was by boat. For miles on our side of the river it was the same wilderness the pioneer explorers Batts and Fallam fought to tame in 1671, along the second oldest river in the world. A river the Shawnee called "river of death." It was without question, Disneyland for a boy addicted to the outdoors. The National Park Service later found this cherished place. It is now part of the 70,000-acre New River Gorge National River.

If you have never heard it, there is no sound like a coal train moving up a river valley in the mountains. The rumble of immense horsepower as the 100 car train works to pull the grade gives you the impression the mountains are mourning the erosion that birthed them. The first train of the day passed our place just about sunrise and the whistle is what always woke me from my juvenile dreams. It took about 15 minutes for the train to slip out of ear range. Shortly after, the drone of an outboard motor would pry me from under the covers.

I would run down to the river's edge and sit there as the fog lifted. Soon Dad would appear trolling up the river in his 12-foot aluminum boat. He would ease the boat to shore and I would climb in. Dad knew the one-mile section of river in front of our camp like he knew every curve of my mother's body. He would guide the little boat, a battleship to me at the time, around all the hull-ripping rocks that hid just under the water's surface. And to all the places the bass lived. On occasion he would match what the best amusement park rides had to offer and we would shoot the rapids above or below our camp to troll the secret holes where all the big'uns lay up.

Somehow he knew when Mom had breakfast ready and we would head back to camp. That's where I learned to appreciate good oven toast. The kind with the crisp top, soggy bottom, and the butter already melted in. Oven toast, fried apples, eggs, and sausage: A suitable last meal for sure. After breakfast I would help Mom and Grandma string green beans for supper.

By the time that chore was over it was too hot to be anywhere but in the water. Swimming, hunting lizards in the mountain streams, and hellgrammites along the rocky shore occupied the rest of the day. The bass fishing started again in late evening and turned to cat fishing when it got dark.

We kept the river camp until I was in my teens. As I got older the folks lifted the strings and I ran the river and prowled the shores catching fish and hunting snakes. How they dealt with me dragging one Copperhead after another into camp and my countless hours up and down the dangerous river I'll never know.

The early morning southbound coal train was there through it all.

That all seems like another life now. Today people are paying big money to "run the rapids" and fish on that same river. Down the same river and on the very waters I traveled alone in a V-bottom aluminum boat, years before I was old enough to drive.

The other day a friend was telling me about bow fishing for carp in a little backwater eddy along the New River. His enthusiasm was overflowing as he told of this little unknown cubbyhole he had found. As we talked I realized it was the same secret fishing hole I found when I was maybe 14. I finished describing the spot to him and he was shocked.

"You don't even fish. How do you know about it?" He demanded.

Later, I got to thinking about those days on the river. And, I realized they were, more than anything else, a gift. Not the kind you unwrap at Christmas or on your birthday. The kind that is given almost without thought by someone who really cares about you. The river offered an education schools didn't and my parents paid a tuition that only cost their worry.

The half hearted attempts I've made at fishing since those days on the river never seemed all that much fun. Driving my own bass boat never matched the thrill I got when Dad would let me steer the little V-bottom. And, no matter how pristine the lake or stream, it never matched the image of Dad and that little boat materializing out of the morning New River fog.

No, I don't go fishing anymore, except in my mind when I hear a coal train traveling the river. The rumble of the engines stirs me and when the whistle blows I drift back to another world. Another time. I guess fishing is different for everyone but I still have the best of what it offers. Memories that are hooked to something deep and running hard.

16 - JEALOUSY

At sometime or another, everybody gets jealous. The cause of the only real butt kicking I ever received was a result of jealousy. Over a girl. For all of their good qualities, hunters seem to be an excessively jealous bunch. Most of this hunter jealousy is pointed in three directions: Jealousy over hunts, trophies, and guns. Just as I am sure you do, I have hunting acquaintances that fit each of these jealous categories and a couple of those that are quite gifted with an envious disposition, fit in all three.

First there is Don. He drives the frozen food delivery truck that comes by every other week. He always has a big buck story to tell but it never involves one that's hanging from the meat pole. Now I don't pride myself on being a trophy hunter but over the years I've killed several bucks that are respectable for the area they come from. Don's big bucks, the ones that always get away, have all been much bigger.

Then, there is Jeff. Jeff is a knowledgeable hunter and shooter and has no jealousy what so ever when it comes to guns or gear. He is quick to offer a compliment for any material possession obtainable by money. On the other hand, Jeff offers no sign of being the least bit excited over any of the far off hunting destinations you may tell him about.

Case in point: He asked about my Newfoundland caribou hunt and after I told him the short version he countered with "I've never had an urge to hunt there or kill a caribou." His response was near identical when I told of the tasty, free ranging axis stag I killed in Texas and of hunts in Africa. Jeff will soon have to start backtracking because he is running out of places and animals he does not want to hunt.

Paul is just the opposite of Jeff. He wants to hunt everywhere and is quick to tell you he would really like to go wherever you tell him you just got back from. But Paul always finds fault your choice of weaponry or hunting method. Recently I was answering some questions from another hunter about a spot and stalk bear hunt and when I got to the part about the rifle I used, Paul chimed in with "I have no desire to kill a bear with a rifle, not enough challenge. When I go, I will take a bow."

Finally there is Ron. Ron has a lifetime of experience with a wide range of firearms and has spent a lot of time in the timber. But Ron has an appalling case of jealousy that spans all three categories with burgeoning aplomb. It has taken me a while but I have learned that I will never own a gun without a substantial flaw, hunt land worthy of his boots, or bag an animal deserving of his bullet. That is unless Ron can somehow take a portion of the credit for the accomplishment.

I guess I have trouble understanding hunter jealousy. Several acquaintances have traveled all over the world hunting with all sorts of firearms and success. I would like to experience many of the same hunts they have and I look to them for advice and guidance on a regular basis. And too, I truly enjoy hearing the hunting tales they have earned the right to narrate. By listening to those who have experienced lively hunting adventures with assorted weaponry, we can all learn if we discard our green-eyed tendencies.

Is there a cure for, or medicine to treat hunter jealousy? Well sort of.

The day after my success on a bear hunt in Montana, my friend John took me to his favorite gun store and began relaying the story of our two-day hunt to one of the proprietors. This gent's name was Tom and Tom, who has taken several small bears and a few more with rubbed hides, was obviously jealous of my success in killing an almost perfect specimen my first time out. His "lucky" comments prodded at the skill John displayed helping me find a bear. Yeah, we were somewhat fortunate but I couldn't resist the urge to interject how "easy" I thought this *bear hunting* was.

When we left John looked at me as we crossed the parking lot and with a smile said, "Threw some salt in the wound didn't you?"

"Well." I replied. "It's the only cure I know for such a bad case of bear envy."

John laughed and said, "Out here we call what you did being a smartass." And I told him that's the same thing we called it back home in West Virginia. I also told him that if you apply it in controlled doses to those in need, over time, it seems to provide some relief, if not for the jealous party at least to those who must share their company.

Oh, I almost forgot to tell you about Drew. Drew is the guy whose standard response to any hunting, gun, or bow related story is, "That's nothing..." Or "I got one better than that..."

For Drew and those like him there is no cure, short of a hunting accident.

17 - TOUCHING ANTLER

It's been said the kill is not the best part of the hunt. But the hunt itself, the anticipation, the preparation, and possibly the recollection are what we enjoy most. While the kill may actually be the climax its duration is so short and the result so final, it can never be best. Most agree we enjoy the hunt even without the kill but lacking it, your freezer will stay empty.

I know of no one who would starve without venison. And repeatedly you will hear hunters say, "It was just a spike." or "Since it was the last day I settled for the fork-horn." Even trophy hunters make concessions when they cannot connect with the one they want. They may use the excuse of a desire for tenderloin but you know, like they do, wild protein can be had much easier through an antlerless tag and it will taste every bit as good if not better.

Many may not actually realize why they settle for a buck that may be under their expectations. It may be that the true reason is too "moody" for campfire conversation. But if you're a deer hunter and you have ever taken a buck you know. You may not understand it, and likely, you will not be able to explain it, but you know, because you have felt it. Not when he dropped at the shot or later, when you saw the smile on your proud father's face. And it didn't happen at the check station when the old-timer by the woodstove said, "That's a pretty good buck!"

It happened the first time, and it will happen every time from now on, when you first kneel down and reach your trembling hand out and touch the buck's antler. That exact moment can never be repeated. It's your time and it is the buck's time. That first touch of antler, no matter how large in size or score, is when you feel his spirit. His wild. That touch, not the shot, is when you make him yours. Your buck. Your antler.

Nothing can duplicate it. Not touching the rack of the big eight-point your brother killed on the old home place, not holding the antler of the first buck your son takes, or fondling the rack of the world record on display at some hunting exhibition. There, beside your buck, with the wild under your feet and all around you, with the sky blue and endless, and with the air sharp cold in your nostrils, when you first touch his antler you feel it. It feels good and it doesn't make a damn if anyone else is watching or not.

Hold it tight. Hold it as long as you want. For when you let go, the buck's spirit and that moment are gone and a memory is as close as you will ever get to that moment again. There is no use trying to explain that feeling, it will be different for everyone.

That feeling, with all the pride, sadness, joy, and pain it might bring, is yours. You are not required to share or justify it with anyone, anywhere, ever. You ended the hunt, you ended the deer, and you and you alone deserve the gift the antler will give.

All antlers hold the same power, from a spike to heavy antlered brute. Never under any circumstance touch the antler of a deer another hunter has taken until he has experienced that moment. That moment, that touch, belongs to the hunter. They have earned it. They deserve it and they must live with whatever it gives them.

Yes, we all deer hunt for different reasons. It gives us an escape from work, leaky roofs, and broken washing machines. It lets us experience the campfire and the camaraderie of other hunters.

We get to feel the bark of the hickory and hear the crackle of the brook and it lets us celebrate and revive the ancestral spirit that is imbedded in our DNA.

But, when you take a buck and touch his antler for the first time you know why you are a deer hunter. You know why antlers of all shapes and sizes are placed on walls and woodsheds. You know why you stayed on stand in the bitter cold and rain. Bust most of all, you will feel.

Some day, hopefully a long ways down the trail, you may be too old and too tired to hit the timber again. As the leaves turn and the winds cool you will remember and you will wish that just once more you could prowl the old pear field, climb the mountain, sit the stand, and hunt the buck.

But, more than anything else you will wish you could - just one more blessed time - touch antler.

18 - LION

"I want to hunt a lion." I said.

"I didn't think you could do that anymore. It that still possible?" Johnny asked with eyebrows raised.

"I don't know. It doesn't matter; I still want to hunt him."

"Why lion?"

"Because."

Johnny wadded up the plastic bag his sandwich had been in and wiped at his beard, leaving some mayonnaise stuck to the red hairs. He looked off into the woods at nothing in particular. "It must be expensive, if its doable at all." He wiped at his beard again. "Maybe you could hunt mountain lion instead."

"No."

"Is it the danger that entices you? If you shoot well, there should be no danger."

"No, it's not the danger. I have done many things more dangerous."

"What about big bears? Grizzly and browns? Still expensive, but doable."

"A bear is not a lion."

"Or buffalo?"

"I've done that."

"Well, why? Not that you need a reason but I'm curious."

"Becasue he is a lion. There is nothing else like him."

"Surely it would cost a fortune and then you may not even take one."

"It doesn't matter. I want to hunt him and I want him to know that I am hunting him. And you do need a reason or it is not worth doing."

"Well, yes, I agree. But aside from the 'hunting' reasons was what I was curious about."

"The hunting reason is the only reason."

Johnny stood and picked up his pack and rifle, mayonnaise was still in his beard. "I've read that they can charge unprovoked, if spooked up close. Or when wounded. I guess that's lure enough. True excitement I imagine. It must be…"

"I've been charged by animals before. Animals armed with more than teeth. I don't want a lion to charge me. I want to hunt him."

Shouldering his rifle and taking a step or two up the mountain Johnny stopped and stared up the slope for a long time. He turned and looked back at me, undoubtedly wishing he could conjure a lion up for me right then and there. "Well, in the end all hunting is the same. A search for something. Doesn't have to be an animal. It is effort expended to fulfill one or more of the senses."

"Or all of them." I said.

Johnny looked back up the mountain and then turned to me again. "Yeah, well. There is plenty of daylight left and it is a good day to hunt." He sighed. "Lets imagine we are hunting lion."

"No John. You can not pretend to hunt lion."

19 - THE LORD's DEER

Lord Rosse (pronounced Ross) stood in his monogrammed sport coat gesturing toward the next room. As we passed by, each of us were handed a miniature wine glass filled with a blood red liquid. "Step into the parlor and we shall have us a toast. I made the gin myself." He continued as he sashayed into the great room adorned with lavish furnishings and a painting of Anne Boleyn. "It is a special recipe made from sloe berries and potcheen [Irish moonshine]." We tipped our glasses and the taste resembled cough syrup as much as did the color and consistency.

When Lord Rosse, the only British Lord residing in Ireland, heard that several American Outdoor Journalist were going to be hunting his estate he insisted we all, "come up to the castle for a spot of tea." After Rosse's gin, tea would have been welcome. We were mostly the audience and he the entertainment, though I am sure he saw it differently. For the better part of two hours Lord Rosse regaled us in the history of his castle, his family, and Ireland.

William Brendan Parsons was the seventh Earl of Rosse. His family history dates back to five English brothers who arrived in Ireland in the late 16th century. There is a rich tradition of astronomy and engineering in the Parsons family and Birr Castle, the site of our little soiree, is the home of what in the 1840's was the largest reflecting telescope in the world.

It, by the way, was designed by the third Earl of Rosse and is within sight of the castle.

When done with us, Lord Rosse announced teatime was over, and a butler clad in a button-down white shirt and jeans showed us the door. Under a vibrant Hallow Eve moon we drove through the keep gate and over the dry moat, leaving the Lord to his crumbling castle and ego.

Two other American hunting writers and I were in Ireland by invitation of Heym. Heym, long recognized as a manufacturer of fine quality double rifles, drillings (three barrels) and even veirlings (four barrels), was founded in Suhl, Germany in 1865 by Fredrich Wilhelm Heym. Heym is now located in Gleichamberg, Germany; a small town about 25 miles from Suhl. In addition to crafting some of the finest multi-barrel rifles on planet Earth, they also build exquisite bolt action repeating rifles, which they were just staring to export to the United States. We were there to field test these rifles and report back to American shooters.

Island Sports, located in Ireland, is one of Heym's most active dealers. John O'Malley is the proprietor of Island Sports and he arranged for us to hunt the Lord Rosse estate. This was possible because a close friend of O'Malley's, Liam Kenehan, leases the right to hunt deer on the 32,000 acres belonging to Lord Rosse.

While Lord Rosse realizes limited income from the deer lease, timber is much more profitable. Rosse considers deer nibbling his young trees a nuisance. Because of this, the Lord dictates a minimum number of deer to be removed from the estate each year. Fallow deer, introduced to Ireland in the 13th century by the Normans, are the predominate species on the estate, however native red deer exist there in limited numbers. On the last day of the calendar year Liam must present to Lord Rosse a predetermined number of deer tails. Our job was to help Liam collect meat for his freezer and deer tails for the Lord to count.

The preferred method of hunting was spot and stalk and for two days I trailed behind my young guide, Mervin Kenehan, Liam's son. Mervin literally grew up hunting deer on the estate and knew every contour of the land as well as the areas deer were using. Mervin was a pleasant fellow who could peel the hide from a deer faster than any human I've seen. However, I found it amusing that under excitement his Irish accent could turn the English language into a roll of vowels as Greek as Arabic to me.

We prowled the Irish countryside in county Offlay from dawn to dusk with a short break for lunch each day. The landscape was a mixture of rolling meadows, hardwoods, and conifer forests. Under dense evergreen canopies we walked in moss as green and thick as shag carpet in a 70's penthouse. Slipping through the misty gloom there were moments I expected to see a unicorn or armor clad knight materialize from the blackness of the forest. Enchanting as this was, during the first morning's hunt I sensed a haunting presence.

Birr Castle

Understandable considering the day before was Halloween, a tradition originating in Ireland and known as "Samhain Night." Samhain Night was a Celtic "end of summer" festival where the dead were thought to revisit the mortal world. Was it the ghosts of my Irish, tenant farmer ancestors looking over my shoulder as I walked the once feudal estate, or was it the fog of the Irish whiskey from the night before?

Regardless, my first of five fallow deer fell less than thirty minutes into the first morning. We stalked within 40 yards of a small group as they fed through a fairy tale looking forest. It was a young doe and Mervin was especially excited for the tender venison it would yield. When my kin left Ireland, hunting was a landowner privilege not generally enjoyed by the peasantry. Kneeling beside the deer with my hand buried deep in its soft coat I thought, "Not any more." Later, as the sun burned the misty gloom from the forest an eerie weight seemed to lift from my shoulders.

Our second day in the field was much like the first; uncharacteristically dry with a heavy frost blanketing the countryside. My last deer, a spike buck or "pricket" as they are called in Ireland, was a long shot across an open field. Mervin spotted him just at dusk as we were watching a ridiculously large group of cock pheasants feeding along a stonewall bordering the meadow.

In all our party took 17 fallow deer; 15 doe and two prickets. Christian Pfeil, Heym's business development manager for the United States, had a brief opportunity at a nice stag but a safe shot never materialized. All of this is now history. Lord Rosse made it a point to show us the game book for the Rosse estate during our visit to Birr Castle and in it a record of our hunt will be inscribed, along with all the others that have occurred on that property over the last 400 years.

After our last day of hunting, our entire party had a marvelous meal at the Monk's Kitchen, a restaurant located in the dungeon of Kinnitty Castle. Kinnitty Castle is located about 30 minutes from Birr. It is where we stayed for the duration of the hunt.

We talked of our Irish ancestry, shared hunting adventures from all over the world, and toasted our health and success. We managed it all without Lord Rosse's condescending personality, pâté, and his medicine-like gin.

Left to right: Richard Mann, Mervin Kenehan, John O'Malley, and Christian Pfeil after a successful morning in the Irish countryside.

20 - NIMROD OF THE LIMPOPO

A hunter can have many partners throughout their life. Special memories can be created with friends and relatives but nothing can compare to the relationship that can develop between a hunter and a dog. Not just any dog, a special dog. Some hunting dogs are nothing more than tools but rarely, with a chance of possibly less than one in ten thousand, that exceptional dog will emerge.

History and fiction tells us of great hunting dogs. The story Where the Red Fern Grows had Old Dan and Little Ann. Jerry Clower told of the great coonhound called High Ball, who was quite possibly an imagined descendant of the real Tennessee Lead. And from Africa we have the compelling story, Jock of the Bushveld, which is a must read for any hunter or young boy.

Some dogs are pets; some dogs are hunters. They are not the same thing. Words are a frail representation of the emotion and memories a great hunting dog can leave us with. To truly appreciate the story of a magnificent hunting dog you must have, at one time, owned one. If you haven't, you have my condolences; you're missing half of what hunting is about.

The Green Greasy Limpopo

In 1994 the Limpopo Province was formed out of the once Boer inhabited Transvaal. It is separated from Botswana and Zimbabwe (formerly Rhodesia) by the river Kipling described as "the great grey-green greasy Limpopo." This game rich country was hunted to near extinction but today it is the center of the African sport hunting market. Thousands of hunters travel there each year for the African experience.

I was first there in 2005. It's where I met Hennie Badenhorst a professional hunter of the highest order. Badenhorst used dogs to follow-up wounded game. This increased the opportunity for recovery when bad shooting was in the mix. Having been a houndsman most of my life, his dogs intrigued me. He had three. Two were in training but one was, as they often say, "a finished dog." This one hundred plus pound hulk of a crossbred K9 DNA was, like the modern Rhodesian Ridgeback, a mix of breeds, purposely – if not accidentally – combined for hunting prowess. During the course of three safaris, that dog tattooed me with the aura of Africa.

His name was Nimrod

After seeing this dog in action, I asked Badenhorst more about him. Removing his fedora and rubbing the leopard scars on his head, Badenhorst said, "Nimrod brings a different approach to following up wounded game. Most blood-trailing dogs are kept on a leash while the tracker follows the spoor. Once the animal has been jumped or the trail gets warm, the dogs are released. They push the animal until it gets tired and makes a stand, defending itself with its tusks, claws, teeth, or horns. The dogs bark and keep it busy until it can be finished by the hunter." Rubbing Nimrod's big head, Badenhorst continued, "From the first time we released Nimrod on a blood trail he showed incredible courage and stamina and brought the animal down himself. It became an almost 100% guarantee that the unfortunate hunter would get his prize if Nimrod was turned out."

I witnessed this on numerous occasions during that first safari. Several hunters in my party shot poorly and Nimrod never failed to deliver. Sometimes animals hit well would run a good distance. Repeatedly, Nimrod ended hunts that would have otherwise been disastrous. Remember, in Africa, if you draw blood you write a check regardless if the animal is found.

During my next two safaris with Badenhorst, I refused to hunt without Nimrod. It was a pleasure to watch him work and the big hound even acted as if he liked me. Mostly, I shot very well but on a couple of occasions, Nimrod had my back. I never lost an animal while with him.

The Baboon

Sometimes however, disaster comes with success. A hunter once wounded a baboon and Badenhorst decided to keep Nimrod leashed; a baboon is just too dangerous for a dog. Well, a common dog. Nimrod managed to pull free and was found, treed next to the river. Without warning, the big male baboon jumped from the tree and landed directly in front of Badenhorst. Nimrod attacked.

They rolled to the riverbank, a snarling, screaming ball of teeth and claws; an indescribable commotion that seemed straight from a horror movie. In short order the baboon was dead. Nimrod was covered in deep cuts and his coat was dripping with a mix of his and the baboon's blood. It was a long and tenuous drive to the vet. Not just any dog can kill a big male baboon alone and live through it; it's even risky for a mature leopard.

The Bushbuck, the Leopard and the Wildebeest

Then there was the bushbuck, a devilishly dangerous animal when wounded. It came at Badenhorst and his hunter, horns lowered, but Nimrod took the charge. Gored and bleeding to death, Nimrod held on until the bushbuck was dispatched. Nimrod eventually recovered and then repeated that display of bravery with a charging leopard, holding it by the throat until a fatal shot could be administered.

The vicious cats of Africa get all the credit for the fear imagined by many hunters but horned beasts like the bushbuck can be just as lethal. A rich Texan wounded a huge wildebeest bull. Nimrod was let go. In the melee that followed Nimrod was gored through the ribs and stuck to the horns of the wildebeest while being tossed side to side. Eventually, the bull attempted to use Nimrod to make a blood puddle in the dirt. Free of the horns, Nimrod turned and grabbed the bull by the nose, holding him for Badenhorst to shoot.

Another long drive to the vet and period of recovery followed. A year later, when I hunted with Nimrod again, he was as potent as ever.

An Unlikely Liaison

On the third night of my first African safari, Badenhorst took me to his farm. Not the typical five-star accommodations of modern-day safaris, it was mostly a small cottage in the bush. A moonless night along the Limpopo is as dark as a West Virginia coal mine and alone in bed, apprehensive and listening to the pureness of wild Africa, I sensed a presence next to me.

Reaching out I felt Nimrod's big head. He stepped closer, licked my face, and then folded onto the floor beside me. In a way, I think he sensed my uneasiness and was telling me, "I'm here. You're safe." Of course, maybe Nimrod was just being a dog, looking for a hand on his fur and a breathing body to sleep next to. Either way, I felt protected.

I was.

All hunters going to Africa need a liaison between them and the wild that exists there. For most, that liaison is a professional hunter, a rough and experienced man who can explain away the worries and guide them through the bush. A man like Badenhorst.

For me though, that liaison was and always will be Nimrod. I've imagined he was with me every time I've been there since. I always will.

Nimrod of the Limpopo was the greatest hunting dog I ever met.

Nimrod of the Limpopo.

21 - WHO AM I ?

An editor once asked me why I so often mention that I am a hillbilly in my writings. At first I thought this a rather strange question and then realized that since the editor was not a hillbilly, he probably would not understand. For that same reason, I imagine some readers do not understand either. Interestingly, a reader once asked me, "Why do you live in West Virginia? Most gun writers live out west."

I thought this question was even stranger and when I answered him by saying, "Because, that's where all my stuff is at." I figure the guy thought I was a smart ass. And, I might be. But that has nothing to do with the "hillbilly" thing. Or, maybe it does.

Hillbillies are proud but I imagine no prouder than Hoosiers or Tar Heels. The real difference is how hillbillies became hillbillies and the kind of person that being a hillbilly makes you. For example, when I was signing free copies of one of my book for those attending the NRA Annual Meetings in Houston, Texas, I met a woman originally from West Virginia. She told her Texan friend, "I sure miss West Virginia. The men here in Texas ain't nothing like them men from West Virginia. When a West Virginia man does something he does it with conviction."

I'm not exactly sure what she was referring to and I did not ask, but I do know that hillbillies are a different breed. This is partly due to how residents of the Appalachia Mountains region came to live there – where their stuff is at.

It was once said a hillbilly is a free and untrammeled white citizen, who lives in the hills, has no means to speak of, dresses as he can, talks as he pleases, drinks whiskey when he gets it, and fires off his revolver as the fancy takes him. That pretty much sums it up. But, how did we get to the point where a description like that typifies us?

The Appalachian region was largely settled in the 1700s by Scots-Irish Protestants. Due to their religious beliefs and clannish ways, these folks were, for the most part, forced into the hills by the more affluent English and French settlers of the lowland coastal areas. In fact, they were encouraged to go "settle" the hills because no one else – other than a few Germans – had the grit to do it. Indians you know.

The name "hillbilly" was probably derived from the linkage of two old Scottish expressions; "hill-folk" and "billie" which was a synonym for a "fellow"or"bloke". Of course there is another theory dealing with the 17th century Irish supporters of King William III. During the Irish Williamite War the Irish Catholic supporters of James II referred to the northern Protestant supporters of "King Billy", as "Billy Boys".

And then there came the Civil War. The clannish ways of these immigrants fostered a profound distrust for leadership that did not originate in their clans. So, they fell in with the Rebels. It wasn't a slave issue with the Scots-Irish of the Appalachia, it was the notion that a Government, which lacked representation of their clans, was going to tell them what to do. My Great, Great Grandfather was one of those. He joined the Confederate Army of Virginia and lived through the conflict.

After the war, as the frontier pushed west, the Appalachian country was forgotten during reconstruction and retained its frontier character. Fueled by news stories of mountain feuds between clans such as the Hatfields and McCoys, the hillbilly stereotype of hard living, hard working, hard fighting, and hard drinking was crystallized.

That "government thing" sort of happened again during prohibition; you can't expect a Scotsman or an Irishman to quit drinking. Moonshining became a criminal enterprise and an occupation for many mountain folk, my grandfather included. Later on, during the two great wars, Korea, and Vietnam, the descendants of those hard as nails Scots-Irish immigrants volunteered for the military at a far greater percentage of the demographic than any other. 44 West Virginian's have been bestowed with the Medal of Honor and the mountain ways and toughness of West Virginians like Thomas "Stonewall" Jackson and Chuck Yeager set a standard other hillbillys were expected to live up to when putting on the colors.

I remember arriving at basic training and my drill sergeant said, "At least we won't have to teach you how to shoot." They didn't. Not much has changed in these hills. Most folks here still go to church. The family – the clan – is still most important. Most folks here have a gun. Actually, several guns. And, they have no inclination to part with them. We still dress as we can, talk as we please and still drink whiskey.

So, to answer the question of, "Why do you often mention you're a hillbilly?" Well, if folks are going to read what someone writes, they need to know who that someone is. I'm a descendant of Scots-Irish and German immigrants, mixed with a bit of Cherokee, who settled some of the roughest, most Indian infested country in North America. Yes, today we have paved roads, Wal-Marts and even the Internet. But, those clannish ways and that severe independence is a hard thing to let go of, particularly so, if'n you don't want to let them go.

Now, if you'll excuse me, I got a fancy to go fire off my revolver.

22 - ARGUABLY LOST

The big pine was missing most of the bark near its base. It looked familiar. The washtub size flat rock beside it didn't. I had just crossed a low ridge and was standing in a draw that had an uncanny resemblance to the last three draws I had been in. In an hour the sun would slip below the horizon, thirty minutes after that it would be dark. I wouldn't say that I was in a panic but I was ready to audition for Blair Witch II. Some would say I was lost.

This was my third trip to this neck of the woods. Tim, my partner in adventure, had drug us to this remote location for the last three years in search of large bucks that hide beyond the reaches of the normal hunter. The first year I saw a spike and two does. The second year I saw a very big opossum. This year I was off to a better start. A nice buck had crossed the ridge about 80 yards below my stand earlier in the day. A little before noon I climbed down and started following the deer trail the buck was using. Some in-season scouting, if you will.

That's what caused the problem. Visions of dragging a monster buck back to camp kept my nose and eyes to the trail looking for the perfect ambush point for this backwoods behemoth. When I reached the point I knew I had absolutely no idea where the buck went, I also realized I had no idea where in the hell I was or how to get back to my stand or camp.

That's when the real hunting started.

Even though the big flat rock didn't look familiar it did look like a good seat. What I really wanted was my sleeping bag and my tent. Or more precisely, just to be standing at their current location. I would have settled for a good GPS and a cold root beer. My eyes followed the little stream flowing down the draw my rock and I were in. Calling it 'my rock' made me feel a little more secure; like something out in this vastness was actually familiar, and mine. The narrow draw opened up about 100 yards below me in a little pine grove. I thought we should have set up our camp right...Well I'll be, hanging on a pine branch was Tim's red flannel underwear. I knew this tree looked familiar.

Up until this time my thoughts had been consumed with hunger, hypothermia, and if my wife would actually take up with the geek at Go-Mart who is always hitting on her. I hadn't thought of a good excuse to explain my absence from the midday in-camp lunch and deer hunting strategy meeting. I should have set there a little longer, collected my thoughts, made up a good lie, and calmly strolled into camp. I didn't.

"Where's your bow? And where you been? Lost! You've been lost?" Tim was smiling.

"Lost? No. No!" I paused thinking, why did I run into camp yelling Tim's name? "My bow...uh...hey! You won't believe this buck..."

"There was no buck, you've been lost!" I could handle Tim's laughing. It was the condescending little grin that was eating at me. I thought about just doing him in right there but I'd had enough of being alone for one day and I wasn't sure I could find the truck anyhow.

"I was not lost! And my bow is back there on my... I mean... that big flat rock. I have been hunting I'll have you know." I couldn't take a week of Tim ridding me about being lost. "I'm here! If I were lost I couldn't have found camp."

"You probably didn't find camp, more like stumbled on it." Tim knew land navigation from eight years of teaching it in the Army. He knew me even better. "Why were you not here at lunch? You wouldn't have missed my famous Jambalaya." Tim handed me a plate. "Here, it's not warm but it's hot."

I was beyond hungry and food in my mouth would give me time to think my way out of this. Halfway through the plate of kielbasa, rice, and way too much cayenne pepper it hit me. "Just what do you consider lost? Not knowing where you are at, or not knowing how to get back?" I queried.

"Either, both, just admit it, you were lost." Tim thought he had me.

"No, seriously...in all your military land-nav glory, tell me exactly what lost is." It was important to pin him down on this.

"OK private! Just like your car keys, if you don't know where they are, then they are lost. If you don't know where you are then you are lost." I knew that was what he would say.

"See that's where you're wrong. Technically lost means 'not found' and to be not found, someone must be looking for you. Just like your car keys. If you are not looking for them then they are not lost.

"Oh for crying out loud! You didn't know where you were, you were lost!" Tim quit filing the broadhead he was sharpening and gave me that drill sergeant stare.

"I knew where I was. I was in the woods for lands sakes. Just like I am now. You cannot be lost without getting lost and how on earth could you loose yourself. I always know where I am, right here with me. So see, you can't loose something that requires no looking to find." I stood up, chest out. I'd even convinced myself I hadn't been lost. I thought I would lay it on a little thicker and heavier while I had him on the ropes.

"No one was looking for me. You were here stuffing your face and hoping I was not hooked to the end of a rope tied around a monster buck's neck. I was not being looked for, I was not found, so therefore, I was not lost!"

Tim leaned back against his pack frame, beaten. I started looking for water to wash down the jambalaya while gloating in my victory over the map reading guru. Chugging down our last gallon of purified water, and hoping the Creole mix didn't do to me what it did last time, I noticed Tim staring at me.

"Let me get this straight. What you're saying is that someone or something is not lost until the search begins. In other words, things that are not sought, are not lost." I could see Tim starting to come around.

"Exactly, see Uncle Sam doesn't know everything" He was probably glad he had learned this bit of information in case...well...he was ever a little late getting back to camp.

Tim continued. "So being placed in the lost category is dependent on another's perception of your situation or their intent to find you?"

"Well...yeah." Maybe I had overlooked something in my hasty reasoning. Tim picked up the water purification pump, took the empty quart container from my hand, and turned toward the creek.

"You know." He said. "I was getting ready to come looking for you."

I watched Tim walk confidently toward the creek in that John Wayne swagger he has when he gets the upper hand. If I was going to be lost in the woods I couldn't be in better hands. It was dark now. Hands shoved deep in my pockets, I felt the comfort of my mini-mag light. Glad that I had a good friend and glad that we were out here together, I wondered if there was any chance I might be able to go find my rock.

23 - NOT DARK YET

There are no more shadows. They vanished with the sun when it slipped behind the mountain. You turn up your collar as the wind shifts and a cool breeze crosses your neck.

It has been a long day, but a good day even without any game taken. When you first left camp, walking along the old logging road, you flushed three grouse who had found lunch in the low hanging wild grapes. You chuckled to yourself as you wondered who had been startled most. Now, they would be looking for a suitable roost, safe from bobcats and other predators.

Then, after you topped the first ridge and stood looking into the deep hollow hidden under the canopy of mature hickory, you found the fox squirrels. The cuttings of the hickory nuts falling to the forest floor as the bushytails fed sounded like a steady rain. You had intended to slip down through the bottom of the hollow to near where the old cabin once stood, looking for sign along the way. Then you would have crossed over the west ridge and eased down to the edge of the timber to watch the 100 acre alfalfa field below. But the squirrels needed to eat too, so without disturbing them you stayed high on the ridge and skirted around the hollow.

That's how you came upon the doe and her two fawns feeding south on the ridge as you eased north. A flick of the doe's ear gave away their location and you eased into a mountain laurel bush. They walked by within 15 feet and never knew you were there. After they were out of sight you turned down the side of the ridge toward the field, headed toward the big poplar lightning put down last year. Crumpled in the edge of the field it offered a great vantage point and a good hide.

You had been sitting there since about three. After eating your lunch, a can of Vienna weenies and crackers, the absence of deer in the field had set your mind adrift. You began remembering a time back in your youth, back before your knees hurting signaled impending rain and back when the only glasses you wore were tinted and for the purpose of making you look cool. A time back when it seemed life was endless.

The grey of the evening was engulfing the field just like the grey in your hair; starting at the edges and working toward complete coverage. To yourself you silently wished you were younger. You wished you could once more cruise the old '69 down the avenue again, play the pick-up basketball game, and maybe even more so, climb the hard hills and hunt the high country. You wished you were not on the other side of the middle. As you looked for another impossible wish he appeared, about 150 yards out along the tree line. He was statue still, head erect and magnificent.

You eased the old lever action to your shoulder. Heard the pounding in your chest and felt your breath rapid and short. The adrenalin flowed again, just as it did the first time with the fork horn and like it did with that first kiss. There were no thoughts of cholesterol or forgotten fast cars.

Yes, it is getting dark. But, there's still some light left.

24 - ONE GOOD GUN

Grandpa stopped the pickup in front of the old farmhouse and warned us boys against any cutting up. The old man lay in his bed. He was dying. And, he knew it. So did we. Grandfather and the man talked. Us youngsters were silent. My eyes explored the bedroom trying to avoid those of the dying man. There were some photos on the wall. Framed without glass. Photos of the farmer, his rifle, and bear he had taken over the years. The rifle in the photos was leaning in the corner of the bedroom next to the door.

My Grandfather had a way with folks. A good listener, he knew when to speak and when not to. He made it a point to visit the farmers who owned land around our hunting camp. During those visits conversation was general with no mention of permission to hunt. They usually offered that freely as Grandpa was leaving: "Ya'll are welcome to hunt anywhere on the place." they would say. I have my Grandfather's love for hunting and the outdoors. I wish I had his way with people.

Cancer had the farmer confined to bed. He and grandfather talked of green beans, ornery steers, and the neighbors. I was interested in the rifle in the corner. I glanced at my cousin and he nodded his head toward the rifle. He wanted me to ask about it. He was old enough to know my youth would allow the curiosity.

"That your bear rifle Mr. Saville?" I sheepishly inquired.

"Yes sir." He replied. "Took a lot of deer with it too."

"How may bear you killed with it?" I asked.

"Thirteen, I believe. Got the first bear killed in the county." He paused and Grandpa took up the conversation where it was before I interrupted.

The rifle was an old Savage 99. I wondered why it was standing in the corner of the dying man's bedroom. He for sure was not apt to use it. But there it stood. Collecting dust and the interest of two young boys.

"What caliber is it?" My enthusiasm was overriding my manners but Grandpa, as usual, was patient with us kids.

"It's a 300." The farmer replied. Like there was only one 300. They continued to talk.

During the rest of the visit my cousin and I traded looks at each other and the old rifle. I mustered enough courage to walk closer and stare at the photographs on the wall but not the gun. Kids just didn't get near guns back then without permission. I knew that. Youngsters today should but don't.

That was a long time ago but I remember that visit and the rifle like it was last week. The gun is not a mystery anymore. Since then several 99s and many other rifles have cycled through my hands. Searching for that one perfect rifle, I've managed to find shortcomings in them all. Often we look to blame our guns for lack of success afield. Rifles that won't cluster three shots in quarter size groups we consider inadequate. I doubt the farm-er ever fired a three-shot group with the old 300. He knew where it hit. Keeping groundhogs out of the garden and shooting an occasional chicken stealing fox kept the rifle and him acquainted.

I can picture the old man standing in the back door of the farmhouse telling his wife to go get his rifle as he watched a woodchuck munch on a lettuce head. If I told my wife the to go get my rifle there's no telling which one she would bring and it would undoubtedly be the one I didn't want. I have been told many times, beware the man with one gun.

Deer and black bear haven't changed over the years. But, today's hunters need brush guns, super scoped beanfield rifles, and the newest hot cartridge to feel equipped. We order up guns for specific hunts like we do meals at fancy restaurants. Options are nice but tend to confuse the issue. I remember Grandpa telling us boys "You need to know your gun."

A rifle is a tool. The old farmer knew that. No different than his tractor or his fence pliers. Never did he consider buying another rifle when the one he had worked. Still yet, that rifle was special to him. Special enough to be close to him while he was dying.

As we left, I stole an extra long glance at the Savage. It was decorated in gouges and nicks and the bluing was long gone at the rifle's balance point. I thought to myself, I'll never let a rifle get like that and 30 years later only a few have. Those rifles are the ones I shoot best. And most often.

That one good gun is hard to come by. The farmer found his. Many of us haven't. His may have come out of necessity. Or maybe he nonchalantly knew what many hunters never learn.

It's the man behind the gun that matters most.

25 - COL ALDRIDGE - LEADER OF MEN

I grew up convinced Star Trek was the best science fiction drama of all time. I didn't know it then, but CPT James T. Kirk was teaching me leadership lessons, I guess through osmosis. If you were watching and paying attention, you were learning them too. Thing is, it took a real man, not a fictional character, to bring those lessons to light.

William "Bill" Aldridge was born in 1947. He was a baby boomer; the son of a US Air Force pilot with time in fighters, bombers, and cargo planes. His formative teenage years were spent in a secluded hamlet of a community called Williamsburg, WV; a place so small and far away from anything, few have ever heard of it. Bill enlisted in the regular Army in 1966, volunteering for duty in the Republic of South Vietnam.

In 1967 he graduated from the Infantry Officer Candidate School as a 2nd Lieutenant. In short order he was with the 5th Special Forces Group in Vietnam serving as an executive officer. After returning home, Bill began his law enforcement career and worked as a patrol officer with the Bluefield, WV, Police Department from 1971 until 1977. He would go on to serve as President of the Bluefield Police Civil Service Commission and become an Associate Professor of Criminal Justice Administration at Bluefield State College, where he instructed on topics like Police Operations and Terrorism.

But his military career continued. In 1971 COL Aldridge joined the West Virginia Army National Guard where he served with the 2/19 Special Forces Group (Airborne) as the commanding officer. From 1975 to 1985 he served with the Army Reserve. And, in 1985 COL Aldridge returned to the Army National Guard where he held numerous assignments with the 1/150 Armored Cavalry Squadron. That's where I met Bill Aldridge and began to realize and appreciate the lessons CPT Kirk taught me as a child.

I once stumbled on an Internet article entitled, Facts & Fictions, by David Weedmark. It listed seven leadership lessons from Captain Kirk. It's a good read and I'll try to summarize it here, based on what I learned serving under Captain – now Colonel – William E. Aldridge.

1. Don't Believe in No Win Scenarios

When CPT Aldridge took command of my unit, Troop C 1/150th AC, it was in shambles. The previous leadership had let morale plummet and discipline disappear. Aldridge told us we were going to achieve great things and he made us believe it. He said we were going to win and we did. The awards and accolades began to roll in, and in a short time we were the most envied troop in the Squadron.

2. Live with Awe and Wonder.

Aldridge taught us to face every challenge, not with fear, but with dogged determination and expectation. To look at our assignments as opportunities instead of problems. He had a way of inspiring his subordinate leaders to motivate their troops. We all wanted to see what could be thrown at us next.

3. Be an Outlaw.

Play fair and within the spirit of the game, but play by your own rules. The Army is nothing but a collection of regulations. Sometimes creating such a conundrum the answer is not only grey, it's nonexistent. When once tasked with running a tank qualification range my officer in charge had failed to requisition fuel for the generators to heat the thermal targets. I grabbed a trustworthy non commissioned officer and we scoured the post the night before we went live and stole – relocated - every Jerry can we came across. There is no such thing as a no win situation and sometimes, you have to be an outlaw.

3. Take Action.

Unlike our current leadership in Washington, who tend to do nothing but preach and pontificate when faced with a problem, Aldridge took action. And, he expected the same from his subordinate officers, NCOs and soldiers. If you were standing around you were wrong.

5. Accept Advice & Make Your Own Decisions.

One of the most brilliant facets of Aldridge's leadership was that he surrounded himself with folks who had special talents. Kirk had Scotty and Spock and Aldridge had his specialists. He was always open to their input but in the end, he took that input, mixed it with his own experiences, and steered the ship to the right star.

6. Overlook Honest Mistakes.

Once during a training exercise I was working in the command center. It was my job to relay communications, evaluate situations, and disseminate critical information. I made a bad call, failed to act and it cost us dearly. At the after action review Aldridge asked who made the mistake.

I manned up and stepped forward. Aldridge asked / proclaimed, "That won't happen again will it?" It didn't. Most importantly, his understanding as opposed to public humiliation in front of my peers taught me something. Something my kids now benefit from.

7. Get Your Hands Dirty.

Lead by example, put your boots in the mud, and be the first one on the bus and ready to ride. And like Kirk, lead the landing party. Aldridge showed up each morning with shined boots but by O-dark-thirty they were as dirty as everyone else's. He would get in the tanks, the Bradleys, and he would sit in the mud and eat his MRE just like a private.

When I finished my enlistment I stepped away from the military with no intent on returning. I had a career in law enforcement and was done playing the solider. In the meantime, Aldridge moved up to Squadron Commander. In early 1999 he called and asked a favor. He said he was tired of the Air Guard winning the West Virginia National Guard Pistol Match every year and taking the Patton Trophy. Being as the 150th was now an armored unit, it only seemed fitting that the Patton Trophy should live there. He asked if I would come back in for a year and help make that happen.

What could I say? To boldly go…CPT Kirk had called and the Kobayashi Maru was before us.

With the help of another NCO I assembled good soldiers, embraced the challenge, and with an outlaw like approach we took action and got a little dirty. We won every facet of the competition that year. I can revel in the accomplishment and take some of the credit, but in truth, all I did was apply the lessons Kirk taught me as a child and Aldridge demonstrated to me as an adult.

COL Bill Aldridge is a leader; the only real leader I served under during my military career. When the zombies come or ISIS is at the door, I know whom I'll be standing behind. Bill is also a shooter and a hunter, and I've been fortunate to share a campfire or two with him. There have not been enough of those campfires, hopefully we'll do it again soon.

After all, you just can't get too much Star Trek.

Captain's Log, Star Date: 20150416

COL William E. Aldridge (ARNGUS) retired in 2007 as the Chief of Staff, Headquarters, West Virginia-Joint Force Headquarters, Charleston, West Virginia, with more than 30 years of commissioned service. He has attended numerous military schools from Jump Master to the Air War College where he obtained an MS in Strategic Studies.

Awards and Decorations include:

Bronze Star, Meritorious Service Medal (with 5 Oak Leaf Clusters), Army Commendation Medal (with 2 Oak Leaf Clusters), Army Achievement Medal, Good Conduct Medal, Army Reserve Component Achievement Medal (with 2 Oak Leaf Clusters), National Defense Service Medal, Vietnam Service Medal (with 4 Bronze Service Stars), Humanitarian Service Medal, Armed Forces Reserve Medal, Army Service Ribbon, Republic of Vietnam Campaign Medal, Meritorious Unit Commendation, Republic of Vietnam Gallantry Cross Unit Citation Badge (with Palm), Republic of Vietnam Civil Actions Unit Citation, Navy Meritorious Unit Commendation, Combat Infantryman's Badge, Special Forces Tab, Parachutist Badge

26 - THE PEAR FIELD

Every hunter needs a pear field.

The thing about memories that makes them so appealing is that they are free. Unlike cinematic adventures and DVDs, they require no admission or rental fees. Making the memories on the other hand sometimes has a price. But, when you reach the other side of the middle in your life, when your hair or what's left of it, turns the color of the bark on the hickory, you wont think about the cost of making them, you will just be glad you have them.

Campfire conversation always stimulates memories. It's funny how the fire seems to draw from you recollections long forgotten. The twist of the flame and the crackle of an oak log can often take you back. A campfire can truly be a hunter's time machine but so can the woods.

There is a place on our hunting property we call the "Pear Field." It is nothing more than a grown up hillside pasture with a lone pear tree near its southern edge. It is hardly more than three acres in size. Long ago this piece of ground belonged to a mountain farmer struggling to carve out an existence for his family. It is without question, my favorite place on earth.

My first memories of the Pear Field are of my Grandfather. I can remember us resting on the old rail fence that runs along the edge of the Pear Field, way after dark, as our hounds worked a cold coon trail along the creek that meanders around the base of the ridge. I couldn't have been more than six or seven then and in just that many more years Grandpa left for hunting grounds on a much higher plane.

A also remember the Pear Field as being my mother's favorite place. It's were she usually took me squirrel hunting and she was always quick to brag about my shooting, good or bad. In fact, we spread her ashes there when her fire went out.

When I was young, just starting to deer hunt on my own, I continually asked the old hands where a good place to go hunt for a buck would be. The Pear Field was always a frequent answer. But I didn't want to hunt the familiar; I wanted that secret, hidden spot others overlooked, not a patch of ground merely 300 yards from camp. The Pear Field was much too common place to expect a wily whitetail buck to hide from prying hunters. So, like a stubborn teenager can be, I blazed my own path and hunted other spots. Often my tags went un-filled.

As I grew older and actually learned to interpret deer sign, I began to notice there was usually a good proliferation of buck rubs along the edges of the old Pear Field. And too, I frequently found a scrape line in November that ran right up the little draw near where the pear tree stood. This small patch of ground I routinely blew through in route to some perceived deer hunting wonderland was found to hold the sign every deer hunter looks for. And that sign was there, year after year.

There is very little "field" left there at all now. Some years back Dad, Sis, and I worked to clear a path through the field so that Mom and Dad, neither of which can traverse the countryside like they used to, could ride their John Deer Gator up thru the brush and hunt the stand of mature oaks that borders the old field.

That same year I worked to construct a tree stand in a large maple along the crest of the ridge and that fall I took my first whitetail buck with a recurve bow. Other bucks followed, some missed and some not. And several doe have come from that same patch of ground filling my freezer.

Nowadays when I go to our camp, the Pear Field is the first place I go to hunt, look for sign, or to just be in the woods. The Pear Field is also the place I go when I cannot be in the woods. It's the place my mind slips away to explore during a daydream. Often I wake from a sleep and find myself there at the old gate in the split rail fence, bow in hand, as the sky turns an electric pink in the dawn of a new day. Then, some foreign sound like an alarm clock or garbage truck will make me realize I am not really there at all.

Then, there are other times when I need to crawl into that place in my mind where all is right with the world and the Pear Field is always there with images as crisp and lucid as the real thing.

This deer season as I wait for a buck to come visit me, regardless of where my boots may be planted, you can bet that in spirit I will be in the Pear Field. I won't be alone. We will be sitting on that rail fence maybe listening to a coon dog work a track or maybe listening to the sound the of the Eastern coyote Grandpa never got to hear. I will see my mother in her red hunting coat with her 20 gauge draped across her lap as she points in the direction of a fox squirrel cutting a hickory nut on high. If and when the buck shows, and after the shooting is over, as I kneel beside him with his antlers in my hands, regardless of where I (we) really are, the Pear Field will be the ground I walked across to get to that moment.

It's the hub of all the hunting memories you hope never burn up in the campfire. It's the place a mind goes when it needs to be somewhere else. It's where you can always picture the color of fall and all that is wild. It is my place. But, if you ever ask me where the best place to go find a deer, squirrel, or maybe just yourself is, I will tell you without hesitation the "Pear Field".

Yep, every hunter needs a Pear Field.

27 - RICHARD's DEER

In the beginning Richard was not a hunter but after marrying into a family of hunters that included his new wife, he really had no choice but to give it a try. Since his arrival there are now too many Richards in our family. There is my father the educator. Me, jokingly referred to as the "hired gun." And, the object of this story, my brother-in-law, the football coach.

Sis did little to help Richard's transition into a family of hunters. Constantly bombarding her new husband with tales of how our father and I were expert hunters, she made his road to becoming a modern day Jeremiah Johnson a steep path. It mattered not, Richard trudged on.

At times when asked to lend advice and guidance I did but considering the onslaught laid on by Sis I was afraid to be too helpful, figuring that when he finally became a hunter he should be able to take most of the credit himself. Richard acquired an old, worn out muzzleloader that was not much to brag about even the day it left the factory. On occasion it would go off, but even then there was a delay between when the sidelock's hammer snapped the cap and when the roar of smoke and fire belched from the muzzle. Targets and animals were, for the most part, safe.

Over the years Richard has had success with centerfire rifles though it has been limited. And his hit to shot ratio is nothing to brag about.

Maybe most important is the fact that he will not shy away from lending a hand, even though his own triumphs are few and far between. A couple years back I took a big-bodied six point about a mile from camp. About half way home I realized if I continued on alone my wife would be collecting on an insurance policy. Dragging a deer in WV always involves going uphill regardless of which direction you choose. Richard jumped right in and we were both candidates for bottled oxygen when we reached camp.

Last year Sis told me she wanted to get here husband a *real* muzzleloader for Christmas. I helped her along with the selection and Richard was more than satisfied Christmas Eve when he peeled back the wrapping paper. I felt I had at least helped him get pointed in the right direction by finally putting good equipment in his hands. Still, I decided to leave the hard part to him.

That fall, as usual, Richard's coaching duties kept him otherwise engaged through most of the season. But, he finally managed to get a day in the woods. Toward evening a healthy doe slipped into view. The range wasn't all that far and the shot, though off-hand, wasn't that tough. But it doesn't matter to me and for damn sure didn't bother Richard. He lined up the open sights, touched the trigger, and the sabotted Hornady XTP bullet poked a hole just where it was supposed to. The big doe ran a tight circle of about 50 yards and piled up. Richard came by the house with that look only a successful hunter gets.

"Wha-ja get?" I asked.

"It's a nice doe!" He offered out of breath.

I walked with him to see his trophy. She was easy to find; there was a trail of Richard's gear stowed like breadcrumbs all the way to her. And he was right. It was a nice doe!

158

Richard dressed the deer by himself. No, I did not offer to help with that either; grown men can gut their own deer or find other adventures in the outdoors. I did help him get the deer in my truck which I let him borrow to haul it home; Sis would have not offered the proper praise had he soiled the back of their new Subaru.

That was just a couple days before Christmas and on the eve of that yearly celebration, with all the family gathered at our house for food and fun, I found Richard had brought me a present. It was the recovered bullet from his first muzzleloader whitetail. He said "I thought you might like to add that to your collection."

You know, I think Richard is going to make a hunter. He seems to be coming along just fine all by himself.

28 - THE TRESPASSER

Small patches of fog drifted above the treetops like lost spirits. Sunrise was an hour gone but the morning was cool and overcast. The world seemed dim and for hunting, he was late. Robert stepped from the car with his coffee. Ignored during the drive, it had gone cold. He poured it out and tossed the cup in the vehicle. Taking the hunting vest from the back seat, he slid it over his shoulders. 16 gauge shot-shells rattled in the pockets. It had the aroma of must but there was another smell, one he remembered.

Pulling the shotgun from the well-worn canvas case, he noticed rust on the receiver at the balance point. That bothered him. Like it would make it go away, he covered the rust with his hand and started toward the old gate and past the posted sign. His keys were still in the ignition.

On the old haul road just past the gate a wide hollow opened and rose gradually to the left and into the rising sun. Covered by a canopy of giant hardwoods, a trickle of a creek meandered down the draw. The path was there just as he remembered. It would follow the creek up to a point where the water disappeared into the ground under a stand of hickory. He started up the path. As the timber swallowed him he felt alone. He had been there many times. But, that was long ago and this time, he was alone.

When he reached the hickory trees he was surprised to find the same stunted oak with the bent trunk. His mind wandered but after a while he could almost see his father beside him. Hat pushed back on his head and whispering instructions as a big fox squirrel fed closer. He could remember shouldering his little 410 while wishing it was his father's 16. He could clearly see the smile on the old man's face when he took that first squirrel. He could almost feel the pat on the back.

He remembered the other times he saw that smile. When he graduated. When he came back from overseas with the Purple Heart, and the crutches. And the last time, when little Bobby was born and the old man picked him up in those bear paw hands. His father had been a serious man, smiles with him were like respect; they had to be earned. Those hunting trips were always special because Robert never had to compete with his father's job, his sister, or chores around the house. He also thought about the only tear he ever saw come from those deep dark eyes, when Dad had to tell him that Mom was gone.

When Robert looked at his watch for the first time that day he wiped his own tear. It was past noon and the sky had cleared. He stood, took a deep breath and long look into the tops of the same old hickory trees that stood over him when he was growing up. When he was learning.

As he approached the mouth of the hollow he noticed a pickup truck parked beside his car. When he stepped into the road a man about his age dressed in overalls, white t-shirt, and a John Deere ball cap, got out of the truck and started toward him. He was embarrassed. He knew better. Had been taught better.

Taking his ball cap off and shoving it toward the posted sign the man said, "I'm a guessing you didn't see the sign."

Robert nodded, "No sir, I saw it and I…I'm sorry."

"Maybe you thought it wasn't meant for you. I've had so much trouble with fellers coming in here trashing up the place, poaching. I don't allow hunting anymore." The man replaced his hat, obviously annoyed.

"I do apologize and understand…it's just, well, my Dad used to take me squirrel hunting up here. I wanted to…"

The man cut Robert off and pointedly asked, "What's your name?"

"It's Walton, Robert Walton."

"Are you Bob Walton's boy?"

"Yes sir."

"I'll be damned! I'm Allen, Allen Wise. I remember when y'all used to camp down by the river. Roland Wise was my Pa. Y'all used to come by every fall. I remember Bob would always bring Pa a pair of them boots he sold back in the city. He always had some chocolate for me. Pa really liked him. He always said your dad was one of a kind, put together the way a man ought to be. How is your dad?"

Robert looked away, back toward the hollow. "Dad's gone. Two months. Cancer."

"Damn. I'm sorry."

Still uncomfortable that he had went onto another man's land without permission Robert continued, "That's why I was here. I wanted to…There's no excuse for trespassing. Especially to hunt. I just…"

Allen cut him off again, "It's OK. It's been a long time hasn't it?"
Silent, Robert walked over to the car, opened the door and reached for the gun case.

"Well looky there. Is that a Model 12 Winchester?" Allen asked in an effort to change the subject.

Robert looked down at the old gun. It was his now. His eyes and fingers felt the nicks, gouges, and the bright shiny steel long void of bluing. It looked rough but each imperfection had been earned honest. It was a finish that couldn't be bought.

The sun was high and bright now, warm on Robert's shoulders and it made the fall colors surrounding the men all that much more alive. Smiling, Robert slid the old pump gun back into the case.

"Yes sir, that's a Model 12 Winchester. Put together just the way a gun ought to be. Leastwise that's what Dad used to tell me."

29 - I DON'T BELIEVE IN GHOSTS

I don't believe in ghosts.

Finn Aagaard was a professional hunter in Kenya from 1970 to 1977. He used several rifles during that time but was very partial to the .375 cartridge and one rifle in particular; a battered and scared .375 H&H, pre- 64 Winchester model 70. Finn kept very extensive diaries on every rifle he owned. Finn's journals included every shot fired, every animal taken, and every modification made to the rifles they detailed.

Finn Aagaard.

The three seven five – serial number 761XX – was purchased by Finn on December 29th, 1969 for 1,200.00 shillings; it had been out on "trial" [loan] to him since the 25th of November. Finn noted in the rifle's journal that the price was "excessive." Finn worked the rifle's trigger and installed a Winchester Super Grade stock. The diary indicates that what appeared to be cross-bolts in the new stock were nothing more than "plastic plugs." Finn replaced these with stove bolts set in resin, bedded the stock, and mounted a Weaver K 2.5X scope.

Finn once wrote, "I believe you should have scopes on all your African rifles, even the "heavies." In the dull light of an early dawn for example, with a black buffalo standing in dark bush 100 yards away across a glade, it is far easier to make out exactly where to place your shot with a good low powered scope than with any form of iron sight." He also remarked that on this particular rifle he never used the open sights to fire a single shot at a game animal, stating, "There is nothing that they [iron sights] will do at any range, including charges, that a low power scope won't do as well or better"

Finn's .375 and its journal.

Some years back custom rifle builder Charlie Sisk hosted a rifle clinic at a ranch in Texas. Sisk's clients were wealthy hunters who appreciated fine quality bolt-action hunting rifles and had the money to acquire them. Sisk's clinic was designed to help these hunters become better field shots.

Outdoor writer John Barsness and I helped Sisk with this clinic. I put together an off-hand course of fire where shooters would engage various life-like animal targets near and far, off-hand, and from shooting sticks. Barsness worked with the ranch hands and built a charging buffalo target. During the two-day event participants would cycle through these shooting stages and at the end, prizes would be awarded. On the last day of the event, after all the competitors had been pushed through my station, I wandered over to see Barsness and his buffalo. After all, that was where all the excitement was.

This target charged the shooter from about 40 yards. Pulled by a roaring ATV, it reached a healthy velocity. The goal for the shooter was to hit the target as many times as possible before it reached them.

To some extent this was a comedy of errors. The high stress pushed several hunters to the breaking point. They jammed guns, missed the buffalo, and even shot the dirt. They cussed a lot too. For the most part the buffalo target made out OK. Generally, during a charge it would take one good hit and receive one bad hit or several misses. But, to the credit of those in attendance, it was all in good fun and those who failed got back up and tried it again.

I stood watching the fiasco while talking to Berit Aaggard, Finn's widow. Berit has become a dear friend and is one of the most amazing women I've had the pleasure to meet. I once watched her out-shoot a number of experienced men using a borrowed, right-handed bolt-action rifle. Berit is left-handed. She was holding Finn's old .375 Winchester and she suggested I use it to take on the charging buff.

This offer simply could not be refused. When Finn moved to America he became one of the most trusted gun writers of all time. Growing up I hung on every word he penned. His straightforward writing style, which was based on common sense and most importantly field experience, spoke to me. His words were void of conjecture and the continued repeating of gun writer cliché's. I would be lying if I did not admit Finn's writing has influenced mine. I'm not ashamed of that.

I stuffed three thick cartridges into the magazine. Stepped up to the shooting point, cycled the butter smooth action and nodded to Barsness that I was ready. The ATV charged off and the buffalo target came at me. About five seconds later it slammed into the bumper stop and Finn's rifle was empty. Berit, her son, and I stepped over to the target. The event had unfolded before my eyes and at my hands but I was unsure of the result and had no memory of what had occurred.

Centered in the chest of the buffalo target were three, .375 caliber holes that formed a group measuring about two inches across. I'm not bragging about my marksmanship abilities. I *cannot* shoot that well and haven't since. That rifle is forever connected to the spirit of a man who had stood that ground countless times before. Some associations cannot be broken.

Finn's rifle did the shooting, I just held on.

I don't believe in ghosts.

Maybe I should.

*Erik and Berit Aagaard, the seroiusly dead buffalo target,
and Richard Mann.*

30 - THE HILLBILLY

Appalachia is a cultural region of the eastern United States. Geographical reference books claim it runs from Mississippi to New York. But those who most often write those books don't live there or understand those who do. The heart of Appalachia is the mountains of West Virginia, which is the only state fully inside the referenced territory. There in those hills is where Scotch-Irish and German immigrants settled, lived off the land, raised families, and fought Indians. It's also where they took up different sides and fought each other during the War of Northern Aggression.

A "hillbilly" is what folks who live there are often called. It's one of the most misunderstood terms and has sort of became the modern Yankee's derogatory description of real folks who live in and / or off the country. I've lived in Appalachia most of my life. Grew up in a clannish family, and was raised by what I'd would call real hillbillies. In fact, the truest hillbilly I know has been my truest friend for as long as I've been walking these hills. His name is Johnny Walker.

Like me, Walker was born of German and Scots-Irish decent. His German ancestors were gun makers, the others were farmers. One ancestor fought for the Confederacy during the Civil War and another ran moonshine during the depression. Walker grew up on a farm and grew up hunting. He grew up outside. Four years my elder, he was not so much my mentor as my partner in crime. My feet struggled to fill his footsteps wherever they led. All grown up now, we still share adventures. Mine have ranged worldwide but Walker's have mostly kept to the rugged Allegheny hills.

Like the Germans on his mother's side of the family, he builds traditional muzzleloaders from scratch. He rifles his own barrels by hand, carves his own stocks from curly maple, and then uses those rifles to out-shoot all comers. He lives on a farm, raises crops, cows, and sheep and, he teaches horses and mules how to act around humans. In fact, Walker has mastered the art of gun-breaking horses. If you want to ride and shoot at the same time, he can show you and your horse how it's done.

He knows how to shoot because he was raised as a hillbilly. His grandpa showed him how, his daddy showed him how, and he learned the rest on his own. I've had the opportunity to out-shoot some competitive professionals, esteemed gun writers, and even some well-regarded trainers. I don't brag about those accomplishments. In fact I don't really consider them much of an accomplishment at all. However, on a few rare occasions, I've out-shot Johnny Walker. Because I've seen what he can do with a gun – on demand when it matters – I'll brag about that.

But his talents do not just lie in weaponry and husbandry. He is a college educated engineer who has ramrodded a pipeline company most of his life. Hard days, hard work, and a damn hard life, where every foot you dig in a day means money in your pocket. A lifetime of driving men who drive big equipment has taught him a thing or two about these hills. He can look at a patch of ground and provide you a geological assessment in minutes.

To some, all those skills might not seem applicable to modern living. After all, to make it in this modern world many would have you believe all you need is a degree, a computer and a smart phone. These same folks don't even know why a fellow ought to carry a knife. But, there are still places where a professional, college educated hillbilly is needed. And, when that type of man is needed, no one else will do.

Through his church, Walker became associated with a Baptist Mission in Kodiak, Alaska. On this little rugged island the mission used to have a sustaining farm but bad times, harsh conditions, and a lack of men with the right stuff pushed them to the brink. Walker felt a calling to go up there and sort them folks out. And, for the last two years that's where he's spent his summers. This year he'll be there for most of the 12 months – even the really hard ones. Every month is hard on Kodiak.

Not only has he brought leadership, guidance, and faith to that hamlet of ocean bound hopelessness, Walker has found a place where a real hillbilly can once again make a difference. To ride, shoot straight, and speak the truth, that's what Cooper advised – that's what Walker teaches and the creed he lives by.

Last summer Walker rounded up horses on that grizzly infested rock and taught youngsters how to ride them. With some help from Mossberg - "God bless 'em." is what Walker says - he took those kids to the range and showed them how to pull triggers. And yes, with his – I'm no better than my word – credo, he taught them what it means to tell the truth.

Johnny Walker is a real hillbilly. He's the kind of man companies that operate in the outdoor industry wish they had working for them. Most don't and couldn't handle the truth a man like that would lay on them. He's the kind of guy gun and outdoor magazines wish they had writing for them. Very few do because they don't know enough about guns and the outdoors to recognize their ineptness.

He's the kind of guy I like to have as a friend. And, while some folks would have you believe there's no place anymore for a real hillbilly, Walker is living proof that's not the case. When times get bad – and mark my word, they will get bad – you'll wish a man like Johnny Walker was your friend too.

Nobody gets to be a cowboy forever but hillbillies – real hillbillies – are eternal.

A true hillbilly - Johnny Walker and his horse, Ranger.

31 - LONG RANGE HUNTING

The topic of long-range hunting gets a lot of attention around campfires, at gun store counters, and in the sporting press. One problem is that long-range hunting has never been definitively defined. There is of course a reason for this. If you're shooting a .22 LR, long range means something completely different than if you're shooting a .300 Winchester Magnum.

My definition of long-range hunting has long been shooting at any range where you have to hold off the animal. This applies very well until you bring field adjustable turrets into the equation. Target turrets or ballistic dials allow you to hold dead on at almost any range. So, this definition might need the addendum of, "with a maximum point blank or 1/3 second zero."

My son's African Rifle, a Mossberg Patriot in .308 Winchester loaded with 165 grain Nosler Trophy Grade AccuBonds, has a 1/3 second zero or maximum point blank range of about 270 yards. Zeroed at 230 yards the bullet will never rise or fall more than three inches above or below the line of sight out to that distance. Given this definition, long-range for him and his rifle would be anything beyond 270 yards.

Another way to define long-range is with velocity. Big game bullets are designed to expand because bullets that expand damage more tissue and put animals down faster. If you're shooting at an animal so far away the bullet has slowed below the velocity needed to generate expansion, you could say that's a long damn ways, at least for the load you are using. With the .308 Winchester this distance will vary depending on the bullet you are shooting and its muzzle velocity. For example, the Nosler AccuBond needs to impact at about 1800 fps to provide meaningful expansion. Using this definition, long-range with my son's rifle, firing a 165 grain Nosler AccuBond, would be just on the other side of 500 yards.

You might also argue that due to the potential for animal movement, if it takes the bullet more than a half-second to get there, you're shooting at long-range. This makes sense too; in a half second an animal could move more than a foot and cause a miss or a wounding shot. With my son's rifle his half-second distance would be 400 yards.

Yet another method is to use the natural shot dispersion of your rifle / cartridge combination. If your rifle, like my son's, averages 1.3 inches for five, five-shot groups at 100 yards, then the distance where this group size exceeds a kill zone could be considered long-range or at least high risk. Bat's Mossberg theoretically has the potential to group outside the kill zone at any distance beyond 461 yards.

All of this technical number crushing is interesting but what about the person behind the rifle? No matter what all the numbers tell you, if you cannot shoot well, they mean nothing. Brag about ballistics, scopes, triggers and high dollar barrels all you like, the weak link is the person the trigger finger is attached to. Not only do they need the skill to make the shot, they need the honesty to pass on shots they know are outside their ability. The good news is that with practice, skill and good equipment can come together and allow a hunter to connect.

During the summer of 2015 my son and I were watching several kudu bulls and some cows on a mountain.

They were about 900 yards away and after an hour or of two looking through one of Leupold's new and excellent GR 12×40 spotting scopes, we picked one out. The problem was the kudu had already seen us and we needed a plan.

Our professional hunter, Geoffrey Wayland of Fort Richmond Safaris, finally rationalized a tactical approach. He and Bat would sit on the tailgate of the truck and I would drive up to the wood line, which was about 600 yards from the kudu. Once there, they would slip off and stealth into the trees at the base of the mountain as I drove away. Bat and I discussed the situation and concluded that, with a good rest, 450 yards was his limit. I also reminded him to set the CDS dial on his Leupold scope as soon as Geoffrey fed him the range.

Hey, I've watched this kid shoot since he was four. I knew what he was capable of. What I did not know was what he was capable of when under the intense pressure of a trophy kudu.

I wheeled the Toyota truck like a pro, even with the steering wheel on the wrong side, while shifting gears with my left hand. In the end I would get no credit for this. The boys bailed out and I pulled about a mile away, stopping so I could see the bull through a gap in the trees.

I waited what seemed like an eternity and then saw the kudu spook and begin to move up hill. The biggest bull stopped under a tree, I held my breath and began to count; 1, 2, 3, 4, 5 – time was running out – 6, 7… He hit the ground, I heard the shot, and then I heard the impact.

I jumped in the truck, grinded a few gears, and rushed to the base of the mountain. Bum knee and all, I shot up the rock slope wanting to be there when Bat arrived. Bat and Geoffrey had returned to the truck so I beat them to the bull by a few minutes. Long enough to get the dust and what not out of my eyes before they arrived.

It was not just a shot, it was a hunt. A hunt that, like all hunts, is ultimately all about the shot; finding it, getting it, taking it and making it. It was a 456-yard journey for the bullet that lasted for about 6/10ths of a second. It occurred in just a blink of an eye. And, that brings us to the moral of this story, which has nothing to do with long-range hunting. It's about how fast your kids grow up.

If you blink you'll miss it.

What is the definition of long-range hunting, Anymore, I have no freaking idea! But, I can tell you one thing with one hundred percent certainty:

When your 15-year-old son shoots a trophy kudu bull, 456 yards is just a few quick steps, even if they are all up hill.

Richard and his son, Sabastian "Bat" Mann, with Bat's long range kudu.

32 - LAST HUNTS

I watched Dad as we trudged along the old haul road back to camp. Years ago it was all I could do to keep up with him. Now, I found myself slowing down so we could walk side by side. Along the way, he would stop and point to an old oak, a rock, or maybe a certain ridge, and then recall a hunting adventure from years past. It gave him a chance to catch his breath and rest his knees but it gave me something more important.

Dad and I have always hunted together but over a lifetime there were periods that saw little action in the woods. Work and other obligations always infringe on the things we enjoy the most.

Once, along the trail as the road ascended a steep grade, Dad stopped and leaned the old rifle against a tree and then sat down on a big sandstone rock. He was noticeably tired. I reached him the water bottle and then sat on the ground at his feet. For a long while we said nothing, just rested there watching the sun slowly descend toward the horizon.

Hunting season, like the day, was quickly drawing to a close and I wondered silently if Dad's legs would carry him through next year's hunt. Or, fearfully and briefly, I worried about the possibility of something worse. When I was still too young for girls I lost my Grandfather who had been my outdoor mentor and sometimes-hunting companion.

I can vividly remember many of our outings but I am not sure I can recall the last time we hunted in concert. I am sure that back then I never expected a hunt to be the last one.

"Fall is my favorite time of year." Dad said breaking the silence. "When the leaves start to turn, I always know it won't be long until I'm in the woods." "Me too." I replied, helping Dad to his feet. As he looked up the path he wrapped his hands around the old rifle that looked as tired as he did.

"Camp is not far now Dad. Just over the ridge and across the creek." I said it just the way he had said it to me countless times when I felt too tired to take another step. "I'm OK. Really. Just in no hurry to get back." With that, we started up the trail.

Cresting the ridge I could see the light shinning through the cabin window. As always, Mom would be out by the fire wondering if the shot she had heard had been ours. We stopped again for a moment looking down into the little valley. Smoke rose from the campfire and trailed off down the creek just above the treetops like lost souls.

I stood there in silence and thought of friends whom I'd shared hunts and campfires with, and how they were called away much too soon. Back then I had expected us to prowl the timber forever, never once considering that the most recent or maybe the next hunt might be our last.

I started to step off toward the cabin and Dad put his hand on my shoulder. Like he was reading my mind he looked me in the eye and said: "Some of the best memories you'll ever make, you'll make in the woods hunting with friends and family. Always make sure you have time for it."

You never know which hunt will be someone's last. You never know which hunt will be your last. It could be the whitetails your son and you chased last fall, the bear a close friend and you will follow this spring, or the turkey dad called in for you three years ago.

Hunt often, hunt hard and do it for the fun. Approach every hunt as though it was your last and remember the details. The musty smell of the forest floor, the whisper of the wind high in the oaks, the laughs and the smiles.

Do this because, last hunts don't tell you when they're coming.

In memory of JG - my best friends father

Epilogue - Shadowland

Shadowland Publishing is a division of Ramworks INC. All self-published books by Richard Mann will be published under that name. *Under Orion* is the first. Shadowland is not some mythical place where mall ninjas, tactards, wanna be gunfighters, and great hunters go to drink whiskey and pontificate. It is however a special place.

When I went to work as a Special Agent for the railroad police I met John Velke. Velke had written the history of the Baldwin-Felts Detective Agency. William Baldwin founded this agency and in time it became the Norfolk Western - now Norfolk Southern - Railroad Police. Baldwin was a self described "shootist" who had a legendary law enforcement career, survived many gunfights, tracked down members of the Hatfield gang, was friends with Teddy Roosevelt, and even did investigative work for him. On the east coast, at around the turn of the century, Baldwin was every bit the legend Bat Masterson was in the west. My area of responsibility was the same Baldwin covered during his tenure.

Baldwin named his Troutville, Virginia, estate "Shadowland" and after collaborating with Velke on the 2nd edition of his book, my wife and I decided if we ever had a piece of ground worth naming, we'd do the same. This was somewhat ironic since our first home - a used 1979 single wide trailer - was in a rundown mobile home park called "Shadow Wood."

If you turn up the driveway to hour hillbilly plantation/shooting range, you will see a sign that says, "Shadowland." Nope, it's nothing swanky and it's a long way from an antebellum mansion. But, it is our home - our castle. It's where we live, shoot, and hunt. And, it's where we raise our children who will do the same.

More than that, it is also the totem for our family's Scots-Irish heritage and represents the shadow all free men should cast: one of hidden armed independence and strength. In his book, **Born Fighting**, former Senator Jim Webb suggests the Scots-Irish immigrants were loyal to kin, held an extreme mistrust of governmental authority, and had a propensity to bear arms and to use them. I see nothing wrong with that description and can identify with those character traits.

Shadowland is also a tribute to William Baldwin, one of the most legendary lawmen to ever chase down a bad man.

Richard Mann - The formative years.

www.ingramcontent.com/pod-product-compliance
Lightning Source LLC
Chambersburg PA
CBHW071348280526
45787CB00001B/253